Dynamic Consultation:
9 Keys to Unity

Trip Barthel, M.A.

9 FACETS

Publishing

Portions of this book have previously appeared in

Golden Choices:

Taking the Praiseworthy Path

Transforming Conflict into Consensus: 9 Keys to Synergy

is the secular version of this book.

Positive activity Interventions (pg 28)
B Good things, Best Future Self

Thank You

I wish to thank a number of people for their assistance in assembling this book: John Kolstoe for his deep thought and inspiration, Roya Bauman for the title, Terry Cassiday for her support, Kiser Barnes, for encouraging me to share my stories, my daughter Molly Barthel, and my son, Daniel Barthel for their inspiration and my wife Cindy Savage for being by my side as I finished this book.

I must particularly thank my good friend, Shamil Fattakhov for starting me down this road. Shamil teaches a model of ethical decision making through interactive theater. His program, "The Happy Hippo Show" has acting troupes in 63 countries. We first met in Panchgani, India, in 2002. We realized we both did similar work, and have enjoyed many joint conferences and presentations around the world since then.

Thank you from the bottom of my heart,

Trip Barthel

Panchgani, India and Shanghai, China

May, 2014

Extract from

"Some Aspects of Bahá'í Scholarship"

Peter J. Khan

From the earliest days of the Faith, Bahá'ís have been urged to apply its teachings to the issues and needs of society and to relate these precepts to contemporary thought. Thus, 'Abdu'l-Bahá called upon Spiritual Assemblies to encourage the members of their communities "to deepen themselves by attentive study of the sacred Texts, and to apply the divine guidance they contain to the circumstances, needs and conditions of society today."

Shoghi Effendi expressed the hope that Bahá'í students would "be led to investigate and analyze the principles of the Faith and to correlate them with the modem aspects of philosophy and science" and advised the believers "to be au courant with all the progressive movements and thoughts being put forth today... so that they could correlate these to the Bahá'í teachings."

Bahá'ís who achieve expertise in a field of knowledge could well find it fruitful to pursue the relationship between issues and concepts in that field and the Bahá'í teachings in areas such as the following:

the dynamics of group decision-making, and the principles of conflict resolution and of mediation, related to the Bahá'í approach to consultation and group truth-seeking; ...

Table of Contents

Preface

The fruits of the tree of man have ever been and are goodly deeds and a praiseworthy character. - Bahá'u'lláh, (ESW, p. 26)

Throughout this book, I seek to answer a fundamental question, one that is at the heart of all dilemmas: How can we work together to overcome suffering, achieve happiness and arrive at unity?

As the former director of a community mediation center and a specialist in conflict resolution, I teach communication and problem solving theory and skills on a regular basis to audiences around the world. Private and public, in both business and educational sectors, with individuals as well as small and large groups, my trainings and workshops have reached virtually every strata of society. Regardless of the size or the setting, all of us, eventually, are faced with choices and decisions that will affect not only our lives but those of our loved ones. The aim of this book is to share what I've learned from participating in these meaningful decision making processes with others.

As a member of the Bahá'í Faith, values and principles are at the core of my beliefs. Bahá'u'lláh, the Prophet Founder of the Bahá'í Faith, outlines clear guidelines for every facet of our lives. He calls upon us to continually strive to do "that which is praiseworthy" as we raise our families, participate in our communities, educate ourselves, and serve humankind. With this core belief intact, I reached out to my community by founding a mediation center.

I first became interested in conflict resolution through wanting to promote peace and harmony among individuals and groups. As I worked in this area I began seeing similarities in the way people make decisions. As word got around of my successes, companies were eager to contract with me for workshops on how to negotiate the choice gauntlet and make carefully considered decisions to benefit all parties involved in the outcome. Increasingly people, in whatever field of endeavor, are finding it necessary to apply proven techniques for clear decision making to a broad variety of circumstances. They want the best, quickest, most sensible, step-by-step method to ensure success.

It's not enough, however, to teach just a rational decision-making model. Instead, I've developed techniques over the years to bring personal principles and beliefs into the process, and naturally I draw on the Bahá'í teachings to do this. Dynamic Consultation is a collection of my thoughts about a complete model of consultation based on the teachings of the Bahá'í Faith and the practices of mediation and facilitation.

Conflict and Consultation

Ye have been forbidden in the Book of God to engage in contention and conflict, to strike another, or to commit similar acts whereby hearts and souls may be saddened. (KA, p. 148).

Difficult situations often begin with conflict, where parties are contesting over limited choices. Traditionally, problem solving was associated with the reallocation of resources — or an economic exchange between parties — and this form of "negotiation" has been used widely in business transactions. In the simplest sense, if both parties come out of a negotiation reasonably intact and reasonably satisfied, the issue appears resolved and everyone goes about their business. Maybe they're not on speaking terms, but a transaction has occurred.

Current practices of problem solving focus on improving the relationship between involved parties — in other words, their social exchange. The desire for improved relationships takes problem solving to a higher level in which the means must be justified as well as the ends.

This book proposes a model of enlightened interaction, Dynamic Consultation. This vibrant process asks parties to step outside of themselves, to consider a broader range of perspectives, to ponder the ethical implications of any given decision, to develop a wider range of options, and to craft a holistic solution that is something more than was either expected or required.

Historically, ethics has drawn its foundation from philosophers such as Plato, Aristotle and Aquinas and has focused on both spiritual and secular ideals. For the past several hundred years, however, economic influences have overtaken our spiritual values as the driver of social interaction. Our modern society has generally taken a secular humanist approach to problem-solving and has embraced the assumption, whether in our professional or our personal lives, that we should not inject our own beliefs and values into the decision-making process. To be rational, the theory goes; a decision must be neutral—devoid of personal bias or influence.

The purpose of this book is to remind us that there are universal values that can be used in making better and longer-lasting decisions. In sharing what this model might look like, I hope to stimulate discussion about bringing those universal values into our personal lives and society more overtly.

Parties in problem solving often take the easy way out and don't use the opportunity to more completely explore an issue or make sure that the outcome is in line with their personal principles. We always make our most difficult decisions based on deeply held beliefs; however, we're not always aware of the foundation of those convictions. It is my belief that, combined with a deeper understanding of human relationships, a decision-making model incorporating the principles of Bahá'í consultation can make a significant contribution to our growth and progress as a society.

Rather than suppress our spiritual foundation, Dynamic Consultation acknowledges our connection to the divine. It is important to understand that the process I'm setting forth here represents one of many possible models of Bahá'í consultation. I created this framework primarily for my own use in mediation and facilitation, where I found a need to bring principles into the discussion and decision framework.

The Decision Framework

This decision framework — which I call "Dynamic Consultation" — is intended to be acceptable to anyone, anywhere, and from any walk of life. I have personally tested it in domestic and international settings, with individuals from diverse backgrounds who have opposing objectives, and in small and large groups. In every case I asked for feedback on the process that might be ambiguous, amorphous or repetitive. I hope to continue to refine the process further through response this book. Please e-mail me with your comments at trip1844@gmail.com. For more information and upcoming webinars please see my Five Keys to Harmony website, www.5kth.com/5k.

A Note on the Case Studies in this Book

The best way to demonstrate the skills of Dynamic Consultation is to use actual stories. The Case Studies in this book are from my experience as a mediator and facilitator. Almost all the stories in this book are from large group work that was done in open, public settings. In every case, names have been changed to protect any of those who might have been personally involved. Each key uses the story to demonstrate the skill for that key.

Taking Action

This book is about the skills of consultation. It is about taking practical action based on the Bahá'í Writings on consultation, the theory of group process and the practices of mediation and facilitation. Each of the keys gives proven advice about effective group decision making. I wish you all the best as you put the guidance into practice.

Authoritative Interpretation

Finally, I wish to offer the following quote to assure the reader that I understand the value of this humble offering is, at best, my own understanding and not an authoritative interpretation of the Bahá'í Writings. It is my hope that, after reading Dynamic Consultation, you will have more questions than answers, for it is our questions that lead us in new and surprising directions.

The existence of authoritative interpretations does not preclude the individual from engaging in the study of the Teachings and thereby arriving at a personal interpretation or understanding. A clear distinction is, however, drawn in the Bahá'í Writings between authoritative interpretation and the understanding that each individual arrives at from a study of its Teachings. Individual interpretations based on a person's understanding of the Teachings constitute the fruit of man's rational power and may well contribute to a greater comprehension of the Faith. Such views, nevertheless, lack authority. In presenting their personal ideas, individuals are cautioned not to discard the authority of the revealed words, not to deny or contend with the authoritative interpretation, and not to engage in controversy; rather they should offer their thoughts as a contribution to knowledge, making it clear that their views are merely their own. (KA, pp. 221-222)

Crisis and Insight

Psychologists say that we only change in 2 ways, through crisis or insight. Consider the following progression.

Suffering, which leads to
Crisis, which results in
Conflict, which provides an opportunity to
Engage, which engenders us to
Empathize with others, which leads us to
Explore our situation, which invites us to
Envision the future, which allows us to
Expand our choices, which inclines us to
Elucidate the principles, which persuades us to
Evaluate our choices, which empowers us
Execute our plan, which enables us to
Examine our interaction, which results in
Insight, which embraces
Authentic Happiness.

'To attain eternal happiness one must suffer.
He who has reached the state of self-sacrifice has true joy.
Temporal joy will vanish.' (SAQ, p. 60)

INTRODUCTION

Present exigencies demand new methods of solution; world problems are without precedent. Old ideas and modes of thought are fast becoming obsolete. Ancient laws and archaic ethical systems will not meet the requirements of modern conditions, for this is clearly the century [20ᵗʰ] of a new life, the century of the revelation of reality and, therefore, the greatest of all centuries.
(PUP, p. 140)

Welcome to our classroom, the planet Earth. Our purpose in this classroom is to acquire the spiritual attributes we need for our eternal spiritual life — attributes that will contribute to our success and happiness both here and in the worlds to come. Our lessons in this classroom are aimed at discovering what those attributes and principles are, and how we can practice them through our decisions and actions. These attributes are acquired and manifested in our inner life through prayer and reflection, and exhibited in our outer life through praiseworthy acts of service.

Dynamic Consultation focuses on acquiring these attributes through living an authentically happy life—one where our actions are consistent with our deeply held beliefs. This is done by choosing actions that promote individual growth and prosperity while serving others. Life ranges from suffering to happiness, and while suffering is painful it is necessary to achieve growth.

This book is about using a Bahá'í approach to solve difficult problems. However it is more than mere problem solving. It is a way of changing the approach and perspective on how we live our lives. Dynamic Consultation is based on a Bahá'í model of decision making called consultation that uses specific tools to guide groups in working toward better solutions. Along with solving problems, Dynamic Consultation also guides us toward a vital and flourishing life. Dynamic Consultation works past solving the conflict and incorporates positive psychology and emotional intelligence to not only resolve the issues and improve the relationships, but to promote human flourishing for both the individual and the community.

Just as positive psychology has moved from correcting the bad to building upon the good, so can problem solving move from short term solutions to creating and restoring peace and harmony.

In this continuing evolution of problem solving, Dynamic Consultation seeks to introduce a process based on meaning, harmony and happiness. The fields of Emotional Intelligence and Positive Psychology show us that we perform best when our thoughts, words and actions are harmonized and positively directed.

Dynamic Consultation is based on Bahá'í consultation. Bahá'í consultation offers a set of unique principles, like honesty, detachment and humility, in promoting complete, sustainable and unifying decisions. Dynamic Consultation incorporates these principles and offers skills at each stage, promoting an environment that is practical, productive and harmonizing. Dynamic Consultation integrates aspects of a diverse range of well-known ancillary processes including facilitative and transformative mediation, Appreciative Inquiry, World Cafe, 6 Thinking Hats and Participatory Decision Making to enhance the consultative environment. The focus is always on coming together for a common purpose and unified action.

Dynamic Consultation recognizes that suffering may very well be necessary for growth, but it is something that needs to be transcended and overcome. These techniques and processes work to transform suffering into an authentic opportunity for human growth and community transformation.

The Greatest Dilemmas

We are living in a world turned upside down. We have tried more new things in the last 150 years than in all of our entire history. Society has exploded with artistic expression and scientific invention at a pace that has never before been imagined. We are constantly challenging ourselves with new and different ideas, leading us in directions that create moral dilemmas and complex predicaments. We have become smarter faster than we have become better so our solutions often have been short sighted and materialistic.

Our scientists have proposed, for example, that there is no need for an outdated, obsolete ethical paradigm that limits scientific exploration. Our religionists have warned that science is leading us into areas of moral confusion. How can we advance as a society if we do not resolve the issues that matter deeply, such as the chasm that lies between science and religion?

Our greatest dilemmas arise when we have the urgency of need coupled with the ability and desire to take an action without clear values to guide us. Solving dilemmas without values leads to mistakes.

The following situation is an example of a dilemma—a problem which seems to have limited choices. When faced with new and difficult situations our brain is forced to come up with diverse and creative solutions. In the following story one courageous person was able to step outside of the box of current practice and see a better choice.

How do we resolve these dilemmas?

Case Story - Child Protective Services, Part I

A child is left alone by parents who are neglectful. Another is physically abused by a relative. Parents are engaged in substance abuse. A life pattern is repeated when the child grows up. The child is endangered.

Social Service Agencies face many challenges in helping abused children. Quite often the tendency is to tell the parents what they need instead of allowing them to make their own decisions. This method generally has very poor results with children hopping between home and foster care, increasing control and interference by social workers and almost 100% recidivism for the parents. In an effort to find positive ways to reunite families, the County Child Protective Services Agency decided to pursue a different path.

Their premise was that an endangered child concerns all of us—parents, teachers, family and community members, as we are the custodians for their future. When a child is removed from the home and placed in foster care everyone suffers: the child, the parents, the relatives, the caretakers and the social workers. In researching other successful programs nationally, they wanted to set an ambitious goal—to keep the child with the family if possible. Their research of studies and programs nationwide showed that when a child is kept with the family everyone does better.

How can they use consultation to ensure the safety of the child and create a stable home environment?

   www.9facets.org/9f

Overview of Progressive Revelation

Bahá'ís believe both science and faith are needed if we are to design and build an ever-advancing civilization. What we need is a new model of reality that embraces both our intellect and our spirit. To paraphrase Einstein, one might say that we cannot solve new scientific problems with old ethical paradigms. God has spent countless eons gradually infusing us with greater and greater capacity so that at this time we are more capable than ever before to challenge the previously accepted norms and reach for a new reality. These changes are inherent in God's progressive plan.

The current crisis in society, with its decline in values and morals, is part of the same cyclical process that has occurred throughout human history. With each cycle of change and growth we see elements of creativity on the one hand and chaos on the other, spiraling ever upward. History is known more for the crises and victories than for the plateaus.

Religion has always been the driving force for the growth of humanity's knowledge, art, science and philosophy. Inventions, art and music masterpieces, literary classics and cultural breakthroughs all followed the appearance of a Manifestation of God.

Throughout history, humanity has been blessed by guidance from God in the form of Divine Revelators — referred to in Bahá'í scripture as Manifestations of God — who have come with spiritual sustenance for our continuing evolution. Past Manifestations include Krishna, Buddha, Zoroaster, Moses, Christ and Mohammed. The most recent Manifestations are the Báb and Bahá'u'lláh. Most of our historical growth has come from the spiritual infusions of these Messengers of God, who have brought us both the inspiration and the practical guidance we need for our continued advancement. Spiritual happiness is always the underlying theme in any revelation.

Happiness throughout the Ages

For Buddha, the path to happiness starts from an understanding of the root causes of suffering. The suffering can only be cured if the patient follows the divine physician's advice and follows the course of treatment—the Eightfold Path, the core of which involves control of the mind.

According to Jordan Peterson (2008), Professor of Psychology at the University of Toronto, the Buddhist saying that "Life is Suffering" can be understood as a reality that humans must accept, as well as a call to cultivate virtues. Viktor Frankl, a Psychologist and Concentration Camp survivor, says that "Suffering ceases to be suffering at the moment it finds a meaning, such as the meaning of a sacrifice."

Judaism and Christianity promote a Divine command theory of happiness: happiness and rewards come from following the commands of the divine. In the Middle Ages, Christianity taught that true happiness would not be found until the afterlife. The seven deadly sins are about earthly self-indulgence and narcissism. On the other hand, the Four Cardinal Virtues and Three Theological Virtues were supposed to keep one from sin.

At the core of the teachings of Islam is the idea that to be happy or content we must be grateful to God, not just for what we perceive to be blessings but for all circumstances. Whatever condition we find ourselves in we are grateful and sure that it is good for us as long as we are following the teachings of God.

The Bahá'í Faith teaches that it is the inner life of the spirit which counts and that people have become so blinded by desires that they have caused all the suffering present in the world. The Bahá'í revelation seeks to lead people back to a knowledge of their true selves and the purpose for which they were created, and thus to their greatest happiness and highest good.

The incredible advancement of humanity since the mid-1800's, with its explosion of new ideas and technologies, followed quickly after the beginnings of the Bahá'í Faith.

In this book we will explore the influence exerted by the principles of the Bahá'í Faith, the most recent of the world's independent religions. Bahá'u'lláh, Prophet Founder of the Bahá'í Faith, who lived from 1817 to 1892, revealed many tablets and letters that provide current guidance for humanity. Bahá'u'lláh's message was one of unity: unity of God, unity of all religions and unity of humankind.

From a Bahá'í perspective, unity represents the highest and most complete virtue that humanity can demonstrate. Unity is, if you will, the Holy Grail of civilization. I will be quoting from the writings of the Bab, who foretold of the coming of the Promised One, Bahá'u'lláh, of Bahá'u'lláh's son, 'Abdu'l-Bahá, and various Bahá'í institutions throughout this book.

Each of the Manifestations of God Who has come to humanity has brought a specific message. Each message includes a restatement of both universal principles that have applied throughout all time, and situational or social laws that apply to that particular time in mankind's development.

Universal laws include love, honesty, trust and compassion. Social laws are practical guidance, including dietary requirements, social obligations and material needs. This book will demonstrate how these universal spiritual and social laws can be used to guide the decision-making process and result in Dynamic Consultation.

Purpose of Unity

Unity is the essential truth of religion and, when so under-stood, embraces all the virtues of the human world. (PUP, p. 32)

The happiness of mankind lieth in the unity and the harmony of the human race. (SWAB, p. 286)

The purpose of man's creation is, therefore, unity and harmo-ny... (PUP, p. 4)

While our personal goal is happiness, the goal of the Baha'i Faith is the unity of the human race. What does unity really mean and how is practiced? Unity is defined in the dictionary as being joined as a whole. Unity is defined in the prayer for Local Spiritu-al Assemblies (local Baha'i governing bodies), meetings as the condition when we are "...united in our views and thoughts, with our purposes harmonized," and when ...our thoughts, our views, our feelings may become as one reality, manifesting the spirit of union throughout the world." (Baha'i Prayers page 301.)

According to the prayer, then, we have four forms of unity: thoughts, feelings, views and purposes. The word harmony is also used, which is different from unity. Harmony is when things work well together; unity is being joined as a whole. Unity hap-pens when we join together, harmony happens when the pieces fit. Harmony leads to unity. The prayer is asking us to do both.

Unity of thought happens when we consider what others are thinking, and agree on the facts and the truth of a situation. We do this through detaching ourselves from any preconceived no-tions and being willing to <u>explore</u> alternative perspectives.

Unity of views happens when we see the situation from simi-lar vantage points. We are standing on the same mountaintop each looking in a different direction. We can each appreciate each other's perspective, and when our views merge we can <u>envision</u> a greater whole.

Dynamic Consultation: 9 Keys to Unity

Unity of feelings happens through emotional entrainment, and emotional entrainment happens when we <u>empathize</u> with each other. Emotional Intelligence informs us that when we empathize with one another our breathing patterns will start to align, our heart rates will merge and our brain patterns will show similar activity.

Harmony of purposes is when we <u>execute</u> in concert with one another. Everyone may play a different instrument but the music sounds beautiful together in harmony. Everyone fills a different role and the roles make a complete whole.

Unity and harmony do not mean sameness, they mean we are positive and open to new possibilities. It means we can create more together than is possible for any one individually.

We also have 3 aspects to unity; unity with God, with our self and with others. We achieve unity with God through prayer, reading the Writings and following the guidance. We achieve unity of self through reflection. We achieve unity with others through consultation.

Unity with God is through His Manifestation, Baha'u'llah. When we read prayers and Writings, we align ourselves with God's will and purpose. When our unified selves work together, we are building the Kingdom of God on Earth.

Unity with ourselves happens when we internally harmonize through reflection. To reach internal harmony we must use the only four things under our control; what we think, feel, say and do. When these four are aligned we have a state of internal unity.

Unity with others is achieved through consultation. When we consult together, with open hearts and positive minds, we can discern truth and take action.

When all three forms of unity are aligned together we exist in a state of spiritual unity. Dynamic Consultation is about the skills we need to develop to bring about spiritual unity.

Bahá'í Consultation

By this excellent method he endeavors to arrive at unity and truth. (PUP, pp.72-73).

Bahá'ís use consultation as a spiritual and practical decision-making process to discern truth and take unified action. Dynamic Consultation uses Bahá'í consultative principles as the foundation for problem solving. Dynamic Consultation is designed to be a user-friendly guide to understanding and improving your consultative practices in order to make quality decisions.

The complexities of the world around us demand new and more creative solutions. We cannot become what we need to be by remaining who we are. Bahá'í consultation is a compassionate, collaborative decision making model that is in harmony with more recently developed decision-making processes, stressing that we are all part of one interconnected whole. Consultation offers both a spiritual and practical path, which recognizes both our divine and rational selves.

Consultation here will be presented in relation to nine keys. Each key addresses a different aspect of consultation and has corresponding wisdom and skills. The skills are demonstrated from actual case stories from the work I have done in mediation, and facilitation. Some of the scientific findings on consultation cited refer to brain function, learning theory, positive psychology, communication, mediation, process design, problem solving and decision making. We must find ways to synthesize the latest inspired learning to transform suffering to happiness.

These heartfelt and inspired keys help us realize that unified consultation elevates decision making from merely a form of deliberation to a joyful, spiritual process.

"They must, when coming together, turn their faces to the Kingdom on high and ask aid from the Realm of Glory. They must then proceed with the utmost devotion, courtesy, dignity, care and moderation to express their views. They must in every matter search out the truth and not insist upon their own opinion, for stubbornness and persistence in one's views will lead ultimately to discord and wrangling and the truth will remain hidden. The honoured members must with all freedom express their own thoughts, and it is in no wise permissible for one to belittle the thought of another, nay, he must with moderation set forth the truth, and should differences of opinion arise a majority of voices must prevail, and all must obey and submit to the majority." (SWAB, p. 88)

Bahá'í consultation is at the very foundation of the modern group process. Its practice contains the values and attributes necessary for making optimal decisions. Bahá'í consultative principles can enhance any group's performance, and can be used in any setting: religious or secular. Bahá'í consultation is designed to facilitate the gathering of diverse perspectives in a process leading to unified action.

The title of this book — Dynamic Consultation — refers to a model that calls for reliance on spiritually based virtues and principles as the criteria in our decision-making process. It is a term I developed to refer to the deeply meaningful choices we make in life — choices concerned with those universal and social laws that humanity has been given throughout its existence. These are the laws that tell us how we need to act as individuals, that suggest how we should treat one another and how we should worship God. These laws propose that our actions as individuals should revolve around love, honor, trust and respect — the virtues we associate with both good people and divinely inspired action.

That Which is Praiseworthy

Unto everyone hath been enjoined the writing of a will. The testator should head this document with the adornment of the Most Great Name, bear witness therein unto the oneness of God in the Dayspring of His Revelation, and make mention, as he may wish, of that which is praiseworthy, so that it may be a testimony for him in the kingdoms of Revelation and Creation and a treasure with his Lord, the Supreme Protector, the Faithful.
(KA, p. 110)

Dynamic Consultation leads us to the purpose of life, which according to the Bahá'í Writings is to acquire divine attributes through good deeds. As we do this we create our legacy of that which is praiseworthy. In this book, we will suggest models of decision-making as vehicles to develop our internal spiritual attributes through the application of spiritual guidance.

The Dynamic Consultation Model is based on being a good person (Virtue Ethics) and doing the right thing (Principle Ethics), without expecting a reward in return. If a favor or kindness is returned (Reciprocal Ethics), then you have the beginnings of a human relationship and the seed for the growth and progress of civilization.

The purpose of our life is to attain eternal spiritual happiness. The purpose of Dynamic Consultation is to promote unity and happiness by integrating modern group decision making processes into Bahá'í consultation. Read the following quotations.

It is necessary to acquire divine attributes in this world.

What is he in need of in the Kingdom which transcends the life and limitation of this mortal sphere? That world beyond is a world of sanctity and radiance; therefore, it is necessary that in this world he should acquire these divine attributes. (PUP, pp. 88)

We attain happiness through acquiring virtues.

Let us live under the protection of God, attaining eternal happiness in this world and everlasting life in the world to come.

(PUP, p. 45)

What is the purpose of our lives? To acquire virtues. We come from the earth; why were we transferred from the mineral to the vegetable kingdom — from the plant to the animal kingdom? So that we may attain perfection in each of these kingdoms, that we may possess the best qualities of the mineral, that we may acquire the power of growing as in the plant, that we may be adorned with the instincts of the animal and possess the faculties of sight, hearing, smell, touch and taste, until from the animal kingdom we step into the world of humanity and are gifted with reason, the power of invention, and the forces of the spirit.
(PT, p. 177)

We acquire virtues when we apply spiritual principles to solve social problems.

There are spiritual principles, or what some call human values, by which solutions can be found for every social problem. Any well-intentioned group can in a general sense devise practical solutions to its problems, but good intentions and practical knowledge are usually not enough. The essential merit of spiritual principle is that it not only presents a perspective which harmonizes with that which is immanent in human nature, it also induces an attitude, a dynamic, a will, an aspiration, which facilitate the discovery and implementation of practical measures. Leaders of governments and all in authority would be well served in their efforts to solve problems if they would first seek to identify the principles involved and then be guided by them.
(PWP, p.2)

We solve social problems through consultation.

The affairs of mankind have reached a stage at which increasing calls will be made upon our community to assist, through advice and practical measures, in solving critical social problems [through consultation]. (Universal House of Justice, Ridvan letter 1990)

Consultation leads us to truth and unity.

Consultation must have for its object the investigation of truth. He who expresses an opinion should not voice it as correct and right but set it forth as a contribution to the consensus of opinion, for the light of reality becomes apparent when two opinions coincide. A spark is produced when flint and steel come together. Man should weigh his opinions with the utmost serenity, calmness and composure. Before expressing his own views he should carefully consider the views already advanced by others. If he finds that a previously expressed opinion is more true and worthy, he should accept it immediately and not willfully hold to an opinion of his own. By this excellent method he endeavors to arrive at unity and truth. (PUP, p. 72)

The unity of the humankind is the goal of the Bahá'í Faith.

O ye beloved of God! Know ye, verily, that the happiness of mankind lieth in the unity and the harmony of the human race, and that spiritual and material developments are conditioned upon love and amity among all men. (SWAB, p. 223)

The most important principle of divine philosophy is the oneness of the world of humanity, the unity of mankind, the bond conjoining East and West, the tie of love which blends human hearts. (PUP, p. 14)

The great and fundamental teachings of Baha'u'llah are the oneness of God and unity of mankind. (PUP, p. 64)

So, the unity of humankind will lead to eternal happiness,

The happiness of mankind lieth in the unity and the harmony of the human race. (SWAB, p. 286)

Their [the people of Bahá] ideal is the happiness of all the peoples of the world and sincere and wholehearted service to them.

(Universal House of Justice Messages 1963-86, p. 246)

and consultation is the vehicle for our journey.

If a few souls gather together in a beloved meeting with the feelings of the Kingdom, with the divine attractions, with pure hearts and with absolute purity and holiness, to consort in spirit and fragrance, that gathering will have its effect upon all the world. The conditions, the words and the deeds of that gathering will lead the world to <u>eternal happiness</u> and will be an evidence of the favors of the Kingdom. The Holy Spirit will strengthen them and the hosts of the Supreme Concourse will render them victorious and the angels of Abhá will come in succession.
(CONS, pp. 6-7)

Positive Psychology

...the honor of the human kingdom is the attainment of spiritual happiness. (PUP, 67)

Is there a greater purpose to life than a life of pleasure and ease? Why are we here? At the end of life who wishes that they had more toys or had spent more time in the office? Did you spend your time as a prisoner of instinct, ignorance and desire, or in pursuing more meaningful activities?

Our goal in life is to be happy, not in a hedonistic way, but authentically happy. This form of authentic happiness comes from serving others. We are here to grow and develop throughout all of our life, to treat each other with kindness and compassion, to search for truth, and to develop attributes and qualities through service to others. Dynamic Consultation is designed to promote positive meaningful growth through the creative application of spiritual values.

If true and meaningful happiness is the goal of our life, then Dynamic Consultation includes the attributes of positive psychology. Positive psychology, focusing on happiness instead pain, finds its roots in the humanistic psychology of the twentieth century, which focused heavily on happiness and fulfillment. Earlier influences on positive psychology came primarily from philosophical and religious sources, as scientific psychology did not take its modern form until the late nineteenth century.

Psychologists discovered long ago that authentic happiness rises from embracing suffering as the essence of the human condition. They see life as a series of paradoxes, predicaments and problems. Life is also full of striving, questing and victories. Albert Camus' insight that "There is not love of life without despair about life," shows the link between happiness and suffering.

It takes empathy, kindness, tolerance, and self-sacrifice to build a positive community. A collectivist orientation is needed to balance our individualist tendencies. Once we have achieved a genuine community, our individual lives will be enriched in proportion to the vitality and harmony of the group. (Wong,1998.)

Christopher Peterson, author of "A Primer in Positive Psychology" (2006) and professor at the University of Michigan, has helped define the limits of the field. "Positive psychology is ... a call for psychological science and practice to be as concerned with strength as with weakness; as interested in building the best things in life as in repairing the worst; and as concerned with making the lives of normal people fulfilling as with healing pathology," he writes. "The value of positive psychology is to complement and extend the problem-focused psychology that has been dominant for many decades." (Psychology Today, 2008)

In like manner, Dynamic Consultation should be as concerned with building the best things in life as it is with repairing the worst, and with relieving suffering as well as making the lives of people more fulfilling.

Dynamic Consultation seeks to determine how things can go right. The process focuses on assessing and resolving difficult issues through positivity rather than treating the symptoms by repairing damage: damaged relationships, damaged finances, and damaged products. With Dynamic Consultation, people can begin to choose outcomes that make them feel fully alive, competent, and creative. Dynamic Consultation promotes individual development in harmony with global evolution. It is used to remedy traumatic social conditions created by lives without meaning.

The Positive Psychology Connection

Society is engaged in the simultaneous processes of advance and decline. Positive psychology helps individuals flourish and find meaning. In a similar way, Dynamic Consultation works to develop the best in people. I believe that Dynamic Consultation will help us understand and build those factors that allow individuals, communities, and societies to flourish.

Positive psychology can be considered from the philosophy of two of its most famous proponents, Viktor Frankl and Martin Seligman. Frankl wrote Man's Search for Meaning after being held in a Nazi Concentration Camp during World War II. Martin Seligman is a psychologist who dedicated his year (1998) as president of the American Psychological Association to positive psychology. Both of them discussed how we can discover happiness and meaning in life. Frankl, in Man's Search for Meaning, writes that we can discover the meaning of life in 3 ways:

1. Creating a work or doing a deed (#2 Seligman),

2. Experiencing something or encouraging someone (#3 Seligman),

3. The attitude we take toward unavoidable suffering [which leads to happiness].

Frankl's first and second ways of doing a deed and encouraging someone are reinforced in Seligman's breakdown of positive psychology. Martin Seligman (2002) suggests that positive psychology can be broken into three overlapping areas of research:

1. The Pleasant Life, or the "life of enjoyment," examines how people experience the positive emotions of normal life activities. (e.g. relationships, hobbies, interests, entertainment, etc.).

2. The Good Life, or the "life of engagement" (#1 Frankl), investigates the beneficial effects of flow that individuals feel when optimally engaged with their strength, i.e. when they feel confident that they can accomplish the tasks they face.

3. The Meaningful Life, or "life of affiliation"(#2 Frankl), questions how individuals derive a positive sense of well-being, belonging, meaning, and purpose from being part of and contributing back to something larger and more permanent than themselves (e.g. nature, social groups, organizations, movements, traditions, belief systems).

While all 6 areas lead to happiness, we can see they both share engagement and meaning. Dynamic Consultation focuses on these two areas for creating a good and meaningful life. Engagement and meaning, rather than pleasure, are what lead to personal growth and long-term happiness. Through these two areas Dynamic Consultation seeks to build thriving individuals, families and communities.

Is More Better?

What makes people happy in small doses does not necessarily add satisfaction in larger amounts; a point of diminishing returns is quickly reached in many instances, ranging from the amount of income one earns to the pleasures of eating good food. Once one reaches a level of prosperity one's happiness is less dependent on income. Earning more does not make you happier. A good meal is not made better by overeating.

In a similar vein, it is useful to distinguish positive experiences that are merely pleasurable from those that are engaging and meaningful. Pleasure (physical) is the good feeling that comes from satisfying homeostatic needs such as hunger, sex, and bodily comfort. Engagement (intellectual), on the other hand, refers to the good feelings people experience when they break through the limits of homeostasis--when they do something that stretches them beyond what they were such as in an athletic event, an artistic performance, a good deed, a stimulating conversation. Affiliation (social) is the sense of belonging when working together with others.

Seems simple, doesn't it—positive thinking makes you happier. Unfortunately, another study showed that only 17.2 percent of adults considered themselves flourishing while 56.6 percent were moderately mentally healthy. Some of the common characteristics of flourishing people are that they are educated, older, married and wealthy. Overall it shows that less than 20 percent of Americans are considered to be living a flourishing life. (Keyes, 2002).

There are several benefits to living a flourishing life. We can also see that a positive perspective increases the good feelings that come from flourishing physically, enhances the body by improving the immune system functioning and cardiovascular recovery (Fredrickson, 2005). Other benefits for those who had moderate mental health or flourishing experienced stronger psychological and social performance, high resiliency, greater cardiovascular health, and an overall healthier lifestyle (Keyes, 2007). From these benefits, a flourishing person is one who experiences high levels of emotional, psychological and social wellbeing due to vigor and vitality, self-determination, continuous self-growth, close relationships and a meaningful and purposeful life" (Siang-Yang, 2006, p. 70).

Flourishing is not desired or supported by everyone. One of the shortcomings found is that positive psychology fails to explain the heinous behaviors in history such as those of the Nazi party, Stalinist marches, Klan gatherings, and so many more (Schneider, 2011). According to Schneider, people with high positivity (flourishing) are unable to experience psychological growth; they are unable to self-reflect and they tend to hold racial biases. Too much positivity is found to cause problems as well.

A certain amount of negativity within the dynamics of human flourishing may play an important role. Using appropriate negativity such as conflict engagement and certain negative emotions like guilt may better promote flourishing (Fredrickson, 2005). Overall, Schneider (2011, p. 35) sums it up with the perspective, "Perhaps genuine happiness is not something you aim at, but is a byproduct of a life well lived, and a life well lived does not settle on the programmed or neatly calibrated."

Amy Krentzman (2012), Assistant Professor of Social Work at the University of Minnesota, defines positive intervention as a therapy or activity primarily aimed at

- Increasing positive feelings,

- Positive behaviors, or

- Positive cognitions,

- As opposed to focusing on negative thoughts or dysfunctional behaviors.

These same factors work with Dynamic Consultation.

A way of using positive intervention as a clinical treatment is by using positive activity interventions. Positive activity interventions, or PAIs, are brief self-administered exercises that promote positive feelings, thoughts, and behaviors. Two widely used PAIs are "Three Good Things" and "Best Future Self." "Three Good Things" requires the patient to write down three things that went well each day and the cause of them every night for one week. "Best Future Self" asks the patient to envision the most positive future possible. This is the focus of the Examine Key in Dynamic Consultation.

"Best Future Self" has the patient "think about his/her life in the future, and imagine that everything has gone as well as it possibly could. They have worked hard and succeeded at accomplishing all of their life goals. Think of this as the realization of all of their life dreams." Then the patient is asked to write down what they imagined. Finally the patient is asked how the dream vision fits within their present life plan. This the focus of the Envision Key in Dynamic Consultation.

These positive interventions have been shown to decrease depression. Positive psychology is about changing priorities to address the breadth and depth of the human experience in clinical settings. Most of us have not had the benefit of a professional therapist. We can, however, take the lessons learned from this dynamic movement and apply them to our everyday lives.

What would Positive Psychology look like in Dynamic Consultation? Positive Psychology can offer constructive questions like these: "What are three things that went right in this situation?" or "What are your hopes and dreams for the future?"

A positive perspective comes from high levels of emotional, psychological and social wellbeing due to vigor and vitality, self-determination, continuous self-growth, close relationships and a meaningful and purposeful life (Siang-Yang, 2006, p. 70).

The benefits of positivity:

- improves the immune system functioning and cardiovascular health

- stronger psychological and social performance,

- higher resiliency,

- helps to create and maintain good relationships,
- promotes creative thinking,
- aids inspiration and motivation and perseverance,
- boosts self-esteem and confidence,
- helps to a balanced state of mind,
- brings calmness,
- you can see opportunities where other people see problems.

Positive Habits

A variety of sources say if you want to more positivity in your life consider the following:

- Each day write down three things that went well and why.
- Envision a more positive future.
- Do 5 conscious but unplanned acts of kindness each day.
- Believe you can bring about positive change.
- Realize that many times great suffering can lead to great positive change.
- The fear of the consequences are always greater than the consequences themselves.
- Limit the scope of your efforts then widen the circle.
- Make it easier to do the things you like and harder to do the things you don't like.
- Create strong social relationships based on mutual respect and authenticity.

Case Story - Child Protective Services. Part II

Despite "ideal" desires, however, the safety of the child was the top priority. They asked me to help them focus on this priority when designing the program. We began by recognizing the needs of children from a variety of perspectives. Through brainstorming, relating pertinent case histories, recalling specific needs and requests of families, and compiling community resources, a plan began to take shape.

My role was that of facilitator as they developed a viable program for endangered children where everyone—agencies, counselors, parents, relatives, neighbors and friends—is involved in creating and implementing a plan in the child's best interests. This program considered that many well-meaning parents face their own challenges around drugs, alcohol, gambling and other vices.

By acknowledging the existence of these situations, all parties were able to design reasonable solutions from parental and family counseling, safe havens for children during crisis, alternate adults to offer advice or asylum, and reasonable timeframes for improvement of the overall situation.

Starting with a "Family Solutions Team Meeting," social workers become coaches rather than taskmasters, and parents and families use their strengths and set their own goals with full awareness of the consequences of improper behavior. Everyone follows the Family Group Decision Making model that applies the following values:

· Children have a right to maintain their kinship and cultural connections throughout their lives;

· Children and their parents belong to a wider family system that both nurtures them and is responsible for them;

· The family group, rather than the agency, is the context for child welfare and child protection resolutions;

· All families are entitled to respect. The state needs to make an extra effort to convey respect to those who are poor, socially excluded, marginalized, or lacking power or access to resources and services;

· The state has a responsibility to recognize, support and build the family group's capacity to protect and care for their young relatives;

· Family groups know their own histories, and can be taught to use that information to construct thorough plans;

· Active family group participation and leadership is essential for good outcomes for children, but power imbalances between family groups and child protection agency personnel must first be addressed; and

· The state has a responsibility to defend family groups from unnecessary intrusion and to promote their growth and strength.

Over the first three years, they saw a reduced rate of recidivism, more children able to stay with their families and a greater degree of self-empowerment for parents who have been willing to acknowledge their problems and create their own solutions with the help of the service agency which before seemed like the "enemy."

The 9 Keys to Dynamic Consultation

Dynamic Consultation is meant to be one possible way to apply the Bahá'í principles of consultation and not meant to be the only way. Consultation provides an excellent foundation for building better decisions. Dynamic Consultation also uses guidance from many other sources. Here is a summary of the keys to Dynamic Consultation, followed by brief descriptions. Each key will be developed more thoroughly in the subsequent chapters.

Key	Goal	Move from	To
Engage	Meeting and Greeting	Prohibitions	Aspirations
Empathize	Feeling and Connecting	Talking	Listening
Explore	Learning and Knowing	Conjecture	Certainty
Envision	Framing and Focusing	Parts	Whole
Expand	Creativity and Diversity	Limited	Many
Elucidate	Virtues and Principles	Resources	Values
Evaluate	Options and Criteria	Voting	Spectrums
Execute	Action and Unity	Disparate	Unified
Examine	Reflection and Growth	Criticism	Appreciation

9 Keys in Detail

· **1 Engage** - meeting and greeting - If you are working with others to solve a problem, devising a principled set of rules, based on truthfulness and trustworthiness, for your interaction is paramount for success. These rules should include the Bahá'í principles of consultation and reflect the foundation for a future agreement.

· **2 Empathize** - feeling and connecting - During the discussion, participants should make every effort to be frank and loving, candid and compassionate, while being actively interested in the views of others. Interaction should avoid conflict and contention. Emotional rapport should be built through positive questions and heartfelt responses. The facts and feelings together make up the total reality.

· **3 Explore** - knowing and learning - Information should be gathered from a wide range of sources, with diverse points of view represented. Speak honestly from your own understanding and listen with an open heart and an open mind. Understand the facts of the situation and explore the reasons behind the actions. This is done by asking open, positive questions that promote positive answers.

· **4 Envision** - framing and focusing - Identify the greater purpose and vision for what you are trying to accomplish. Create a balanced, positive, future-focused frame. A frame is a broader statement of the problem that allows for a wider range of solutions.

· **5 Expand** - creativity and diversity - Create a diverse, positive and creative set of choices. Positive thinking helps create more choices and more choices lead to better decisions. Ideas presented become the property of the group. This means that ideas do not stay the property of an individual or constituency. This allows for the free flow of discussion of an idea without a retained ownership that needs to be defended.

· **6 Elucidate** - virtues, principles and reciprocity - Identify the spiritual principles, as well as the other decision making criteria, needed to evaluate the choices.

· **7 Evaluate** - options and criteria - Compare your choices with your principles and other positive criteria, including resources, and relationships.

· **8 Execute** - unity and action - Taking collective action to resolve the issues, repair the relationships, promote positivity and create harmony. The group strives for consensus, however a majority vote can be taken to bring about a conclusion and make the decision. Once a decision is made, it is incumbent on the entire group to act on it with unity — regardless of how many supported the idea.

· **9 Examine** - reflection and growth - Reflect on your decisions and actions and consider what went well and what you would change. Consider the effects of your consultation in relation to the implementation of the decision. Consider how you would improve both your consultation and your actions in the future.

Dynamic Consultation in Action

Consultation is often seen as a milieu of attributes and attitudes. Dynamic Consultation is one way to create a practical set of skills that are consistent with this milieu. Knowledge says "I know this"; a skill says "I can do this." Dynamic Consultation offers the opportunity to acquire practical skills for both your personal and professional life.

A skill is defined as ability or capacity acquired through deliberate, systematic, and sustained effort to smoothly and adaptively carry out complex activities or job functions involving cognitive skills, technical skills and/or interpersonal skills.

Cognitive skills teach how to think, interpersonal skills teach how to relate to others and technical skills teach how to make or do something. Dynamic Consultation teaches both cognitive and interpersonal skills. Cognitive skills include analysis, evaluation, synthesis, extrapolation and conceptualization. Interpersonal skills include rapport, compassion, emotional intelligence and empathy. Technical skills include making, creating, practicing things through ability and action.

Knowledge often doesn't go beyond the examination, but skills are transferable outside of the classroom (they don't go away when you walk out the door). Skills are knowledge in action and when they benefit humankind they create unity. The skills of Dynamic Consultation fall into the nine keys listed in the table below.

9 Keys	9 Key Skills with Questions
Engage	Process - What process should we adopt? Behavior - What behaviors do we expect?
Empathize	Listening - How can we listen first? Caring - How can we respond with love?
Explore	Powers - How can we use our spirit and senses? Questions - How can we ask better questions?
Envision	Vision - What is the big picture? Framing - How can we work together to ....?
Expand	Brainstorm - How can we increase our choices? Reciprocity - What will we do for each other?
Elucidate	Wisdom - What does society say? Value Scan - What values are important to us?
Evaluate	Matrix - How can we use our criteria and options? Spectrums - How do we feel about our options?
Execute	Deeds - How can we take action? Unity - How can we work as one?
Examine	Reflection - What worked? Enhance - How can we improve next time?

GENDER AND CULTURE

Two final considerations as we engage in consultation are gender and culture. We need to consider how we can promote the highest levels of consultation with all people. With both gender and culture, we need to be careful not to stereotype and think of these insights only as qualities that anyone might possess. If we use these observations we can have a more complete discussion.

Culture

It is my hope that this standard of the oneness of the world of humanity may be upraised with the utmost solidity so that the Orient and Occident may become perfectly reconciled and attain complete intercommunication, the hearts of the East and West become united and attracted, real union become unveiled, the light of guidance shine, divine effulgences be seen day by day so that the world of humanity may find complete tranquility, the eternal happiness of man become evident and the hearts of the people of the world be as mirrors in which the rays of the Sun of Reality may be reflected. Consequently, it is my request that you should strive so that the light of reality may shine and the everlasting felicity of the world of man become apparent. (PUP, 7:7)

Cultural perspectives also come into play in consultation. We must always remember that culture is the word which summarizes the properties of a group. For an individual, these same properties would be called behavior. Reconciling the worldviews of individuals from different cultures is usually referred to as cultural awareness, but it has much more to do with their personalities than their community. We mistakenly believe that someone will react and behave the same way toward us as we react and behave towards them. We don't always get the response that we expect.

Geography of Thought compares studies from Western and Asian cultures and offers some very interesting insights. Some of these are summarized in the table below. To be truly cross cultural we need to engage all the cultures in the room.

Dynamic Consultation: 9 Keys to Unity

9 Keys	Asian	Western
Engage	Attribute behavior to context	Universal rules for behavior
	Compromised based	Rule based
Empathize	Achieve harmony within a network of supportive social relationships	Achieve work related project or goal
Explore	Issues complex, subjective and intertwined	Issues are simple, objective and fragmentable
	Set context and ask how	Set causes and asks why
	See relationships among events	Able to disentangle an object from its surroundings
Envision	See the big picture and see objects in relation to their environment	Focus on objects and see fewer relationships
	Sees the whole	Sees the parts
Expand	Able to entertain contradictory propositions - seek "Middle Way"	Formal logic - seek correct way
Elucidate	Obedience, kindness	Honesty, independence
Evaluate	Avoid controversy and debate	Believe in rhetoric of argumentation
Execute	Agreements can change based on circumstances	Agreements are binding
	Collective action	Individual action
Examine	Drive for self-improvement	Feel good about the self

Gender

When the two wings... become equivalent in strength, enjoying the same prerogatives, the flight of man will be exceedingly lofty and extraordinary. (PUP, p. 375)

That men and women differ from one another in certain character-istics and functions is an inescapable fact of nature and makes possible their complementary roles in certain areas of the life of society; but it is significant that 'Abdu'l-Bahá has stated that in this Dispensation 'Equality of men and women, except in some negligible instances, has been fully and categorically announced.' (KA, p. 7)

We also need to consider the effects of gender in our consultations. While we believe that men and women are equal, we recognize that they are not the same.

Women have seven language centers in their brains and men have only one. Women have about 50% more cross hemispheric connections in their brains than men do. Women can remember about 50% more from a visual scene than men can. Women have twice the endurance, seek advice and offer suggestions. Men like to act and will only ask for help after they have done everything they can on their own. (Gray, 2008)

Women will question a dangerous situation!

Back country skiing is a dangerous sport that involves being carried to a mountaintop via helicopter. When women and men ski together, there are about 70% fewer fatalities than when men ski with other men. One theory is that men will never question another man's courage, but women will ask "Is this too dangerous?" giving the men permission to step aside from potential calamity.

The following insights on gender roles were gleaned from Men are from Mars, Women are from Venus by John Gray.

Dynamic Consultation: 9 Keys to Unity

9 Keys	Female	Male
Engage	Cooperation, consistency, routine	Process structure, competition, efficiency
	Primary Love needs Caring, Understanding, Respect, Devotion, Validation, Reassurance	Primary love needs Trust, Acceptance, Appreciation, Admiration, Approval, Encouragement
Empathize	Women feel an instinctive need to talk about what's bothering them.	Men pull away and silently think about what's bothering them.
	Memory and emotion are in the same brain hemisphere and are stronger, emotions enhance memory.	Memory and emotion in different brain hemispheres, emotions have less effect on memory.
Explore	Relationships, shared responsibility, multitask	Facts, problem solving, single focus
	Under stress take in more information.	Under stress focus on most important thing
Envision	Women excel at integrating, assimilating	Men excel at processing, analyzing
Expand	Cautious	Risk
Elucidate	Safety, beauty	Viability, accountability
Evaluate	Women are motivated when they feel cherished.	Men are motivated when they feel needed.
Execute	Collaboration, long term, unconditional giving	Results, goal setting, project oriented, bottom line
	Women inspire men to act by providing meaningful foundation.	Men can have great vision. Men inspire women through action.
Examine	A women's sense of self is defined through her feelings and the quality of her relationships.	A man's sense of self is defined through his ability to achieve results.

An Integration of Compatible Group Processes

There are a variety of group decision making processes that we can draw from to help leverage the power of consultation. There are many methods that use a positive approach to difficult situations. The National Conference on Dialogue and Deliberation (NCDD) lists close to 400 different models for dialogue.

Dynamic Consultation integrates the practices from these processes to reinforce and strengthen group decision making. We will consider which facets of each of these we can use in the Dynamic Consultation process.

Dynamic Consultation draws from these Processes and each will be more fully explained in upcoming sections. Here are some of the key points from each:

Facilitative Mediation uses honest exchanges and creative problem solving.

World Cafe promotes positive discussions by exploring questions that matter and sharing collective discoveries.

Appreciative Inquiry builds on what is working and designs whole system solutions.

6 Thinking Hats uses our whole brain, with feelings, ideas and evaluations as the keys.

Quaker Meeting uses a spiritually based 3 meeting process to make decisions, where the first meeting introduces the idea, the second for discussion and the third for decision.

Participatory Decision Making builds consensus by creating and clarifying ideas through spectrums.

Future Search observes that it takes 2 periods of sleep to assimilate change.

Open Space allows questions and interest to drive discussions.

Transformative Mediation focuses on empathy and understanding through recognition and empowerment.

Facilitative Mediation

There are many different variations of mediation processes and forms of practice. Attorneys and judges might be very direct with suggestions or advice. Therapists might focus on healing. Facilitative Mediators promote positive interaction to develop choices. Transformative Mediators work to rebuild relationships through recognition and empowerment.

The traditional definition of mediation might say that a mediator is a neutral third party who assists 2 or more individuals in discussing difficult issues, exploring possible choices and crafting meaningful agreements. The process might include:

Ground rules - letting the parties set fair rules for discussion and decision making.

Questions - allowing parties to understand what each is saying

Storytelling - expressing the facts in an open, honest and sincere way

Framing - defining the issues collectively in future focused terms

Options - helping the parties create choices

Criteria - agreeing on how to judge a good decision.

Selection - deciding which options best meet the criteria

Agreement - sustainable, specific, complete and positive

Appreciative Inquiry

Appreciative Inquiry (from AI Commons) focuses on what is working in any system or environment in these five steps.

1. **DEFINE** - the topic of inquiry from an AI perspective. "How would staff interact if all were being cooperative and treating each other like customers?"

2. **DISCOVER** - People work in pairs to tell stories of their past and current exceptional experiences about the topic of the inquiry.

3. **DREAM** - People recall and identify the themes operating that contributed to the peak experience. Themes are the resources, behaviors, emotions feelings of the people at the time of the peak, memorable experience.

4. **DESIGN** - People write how the organization functions if the themes were operating to the maximum, in the present.

5. **DELIVER** - People commit, offer, or request ideas to implement goals set forth in the DESIGN phase.

In his article, Appreciative Inquiry as an Organizational Development Tool, Charles Martinez describes the difference between the problem solving and appreciative inquiry methods (Martinez, 2002).

The traditional steps in problem solving are:

1. Identify the problem.

2. Conduct an analysis of the causes.

3. Analyze possible solutions.

4. Plan some action or treatment.

The steps in AI are different:

1. Appreciate and value the best of what is.

2. Envision what might be.

3. Dialogue about what should be.

4. Innovate and create what will be.

Coming from the field of dispute resolution, we can clearly see how the power of reframing the situation from a problem that needs to be solved and extinguished into a challenge that will be overcome by seeking out our strengths can really play an important role in ensuring that the change or interventions developed will be effective and sustainable.

We will see later how AI is integrated into Dynamic Consultation and promotes a more positive atmosphere.

World Cafe

In World Cafe people sit at tables of four and change tables twice during the discussion. It has seven steps that participants in Dynamic Consultation could use (from worldcafe.org).

1) **Set the Context** - Knowing the purpose and parameters of your meeting enables you to consider and choose the most important elements to realize your goals.

2) **Create Hospitable Space** - When people feel comfortable to be themselves, they do their most creative thinking, speaking, and listening. In particular, consider how your invitation and your physical setup contribute to creating a welcoming atmosphere.

3) **Explore Questions that Matter** - Knowledge emerges in response to compelling questions. Find questions that are relevant to the real-life concerns of the group. Powerful questions that "travel well" help attract collective energy, insight, and action as they move throughout a system.

4) **Encourage Everyone's Contribution** - Most people don't only want to participate, they want to actively contribute to making a difference. It is important to encourage everyone in your meeting to contribute their ideas and perspectives.

5) **Connect Diverse Perspectives** - The opportunity to move between tables, meet new people, actively contribute your thinking, and link the essence of your discoveries to ever-widening circles of thought is one of the distinguishing characteristics of the Café. As participants carry key ideas or themes to new tables, they exchange perspectives, greatly enriching the possibility for surprising new insights.

6) **Listen together for Patterns and Insights** - Listening is a gift we give to one another. Through practicing shared listening and paying attention to themes, patterns and insights, we begin to sense a connection to the larger whole. Encourage people to listen for what is not being spoken along with what is being shared.

7) **Share Collective Discoveries** - Conversations held at one table reflect a pattern of wholeness that connects with the conversations at the other tables. The last phase of the Café, often called the "harvest", involves making this pattern of wholeness visible to everyone in a large group conversation. Invite a few minutes of silent reflection on the patterns, themes and deeper questions experienced in the small group conversations and call them out to share with the larger group. Make sure you have a way to capture the harvest - working with a graphic recorder is recommended.

Six Thinking Hats

6 Thinking Hats (deBono) is designed to promote harmonious thinking by asking everyone to use the same parts of their brain (wear the same "hats") at the same time.

- **Information**: (White) - considering purely what information is available, what are the facts?

- **Emotions** (Red) - intuitive or instinctive gut reactions or statements of emotional feeling.

- **Discernment** (Black) - logic applied to identifying reasons to be cautious and conservative

- **Optimistic** response (Yellow) - logic applied to identifying benefits, seeking harmony

- **Creativity** (Green) - statements of provocation and investigation, seeing where a thought goes.

- **Process** (Blue) - sets process guidelines but does not offer any recommendations for specific rules.

There are two rules in 6 Thinking Hats:

1.) Everyone agrees to wear the same hat at the same time, and

2.) Only the facilitator can call for a change in hats.

Six Thinking Hats works best when everyone is able to wear the yellow and black hats and each sees the reasons an idea will work and the challenges it presents. The red hat allows individual feelings to be expressed and it works best with a single word.

Process Comparison

When we consider these four processes together with Dynamic Consultation, we end up with the following comparison at each stage:

Dynamic Consultation	Facilitative Mediation	World Cafe	Appreciative Inquiry	6 Hats
Engage	Ground Rules	Context Space		Blue
Empathize	Questions	Questions	Discover	Red
Explore	Storytelling Issues	Contributions		White
Envision	Frame	Define		
Expand	Options	Perspective	Dream	Green
Elucidate	Criteria			
Evaluate	Selection	Pattern	Design	Yellow Black
Execute	Agreement	Discovery	Deliver	
Examine				

ENGAGE

Key	Goal	Move from	To
Engage	Meeting and Greeting	Prohibitions	Aspirations

If you are working with others to solve a problem, devising a principled set of rules, based on truthfulness and trustworthiness, for your interaction is paramount for success. These rules should include the Bahá'í principles of consultation and reflect the foundation for a future agreement. They should focus on both the process and the expected behaviors of the parties.

Bahá'í Writings

The prime requisites for them that take counsel together are: purity of motive, radiance of spirit, detachment from all else save God, attraction to His Divine Fragrances, humility and lowliness amongst His loved ones, patience and long-suffering in difficulties and servitude to His exalted Threshold.
Should they be graciously aided to acquire these attributes, victory from the unseen Kingdom of Bahá shall be vouchsafed to them.
(SWAB, 87)

I would therefore strongly urge those who are called upon to make such a decision to approach this highly involved and ever-recurring problem with the spirit of humble prayer, and earnest consultation, and to refrain from drawing rigidly the line of demarcation except on such occasions when the interests of the Cause absolutely demand it. (BA, 90)

God has given man the eye of investigation by which he may see and recognize truth. Each human creature has individual endowment, power and responsibility in the creative plan of God. (PUP, p. 293)

The Manifestations of God, on the other hand, affirm that differences are demonstrably and indisputably innate, and that "We have caused some of you to excel others" is a proven and inescapable fact. It is certain that human beings are, by their very nature, different one from the other... It is therefore clear that the disparity among individuals is due to differences of degree which are innate. (ED, pp. 258-259)

He has endowed man with ears that he may hear the message of reality and conferred upon him the gift of reason by which he may discover things for himself. Man is not intended to see through the eyes of another, hear through another's ears nor comprehend with another's brain. Therefore, depend upon your own reason and judgment and adhere to the outcome of your own investigation; otherwise, you will be utterly submerged in the sea of ignorance and deprived of all the bounties of God. (PUP, p. 293)

O SON OF SPIRIT!

The best beloved of all things in My sight is Justice; turn not away therefrom if thou desirest Me, and neglect it not that I may confide in thee. By its aid thou shalt see with thine own eyes and not through the eyes of others, and shalt know of thine own knowledge and not through the knowledge of thy neighbor. Ponder this in thy heart; how it behooveth thee to be. Verily justice is My gift to thee and the sign of My loving-kindness. Set it then before thine eyes. (HW Arabic, 2)

In conclusion, the Bahá'í Writings tell us that:
- We begin by setting our intention and reflecting on our relationship with God.
- We should be patient, humble and detached.
- We are all different from one another
- We all understand the world in our own unique way.
- We should depend on our own reason and judgment
- We should know through our own knowledge and not rely on what someone else thinks.

Case Story - The Right Side of the Tracks. Part I

One hundred fifty years ago a small town sprang up. The citizens of the town rejoiced when the railroad decided to come through, offering it economic opportunity and access to the outside world. The railroad and the town both flourished.

Nowadays, however, the constant noise of trains and the bifurcation of the town cause conflict. What to do with the working train tracks that passed through the middle of town? The tracks and the town had grown up around each other. They both had historical and practical significance. Some people thought that the tracks were fine and, in fact part of the atmosphere of the town. Leave them alone, they said. Others thought the tracks were a noise and safety hazard and wanted the city to raise the funds to lower them into the ground.

Inappropriate, expensive, unimportant.

Polluting, endangering, outdated.

Neither side was listening to the other.

I was asked to come in and help. Most of problem resolution involves listening, so I set up a way for people to listen to one another. We had a large public forum with about 250 concerned people that was televised.

What ground rules would you use for a large meeting with angry and frustrated citizens? How would you structure the meeting? To find out how things turned out, see the conclusion at the end of this chapter.

MEETING AND GREETING

These are the basic premises before sitting down to consult. Spiritually, they are easy to agree on. Practically, humans are all different and consultation runs smoother when we acknowledge those differences and make sure that learning takes place in a variety of ways. Providing "something for everyone" really is a dynamic way to increase participation and satisfaction in the outcome of any problem solving session.

When we think about the train track issue mentioned at the beginning of this chapter, there were 250 very different people involved, each with his/her own needs/biases/history about the situation. In addition, there was the added stress of thousands of viewers sitting at home steaming up as they watched the proceedings on TV. It is essential to understand the ways the people take in information when dealing with any situation that needs improvement and resolution.

How do we learn?

Each of us perceives the world in a different way and most difficulties are caused by these differences in perception. Learning theory can help us understand these different ways we perceive the world. When we allow for these differences in perception in our communication, we eliminate barriers and allow individuals and groups to become more productive.

The first step in consultation is to derive an understanding of the situation from your own perspective and then compare it to that of other individuals in the group. The following theories on brain function and information processing come from 4MAT: Teaching to Learning Styles. They help us see how we each use our own unique abilities to perceive any given situation.

The first step in understanding is how we communicate with the world around us. We all perceive the world in our own unique way, so to communicate completely we need to use all three modalities (seeing, listening and movement).

33% of us learn by seeing and imagining.

24% of us learn by listening and verbalizing.

14% of us learn by doing and manipulating.

29% of us learn with more than one modality.

Our left-brain mode likes structure and sequence. Our right-brain mode likes random patterns, is visual-spatial, is emotional and looks at the big picture.

Modality	Application
Visual	Flip charts, maps, drawings, pictures, lighting
Auditory	Music, song, clear acoustics, silence, poetry, spoken word
Somatic	Movement, tactile activity
Emotional	Interpersonal contact
Spiritual	Prayer, reflection

Studies have shown that communication is

7% words,

38% tone and

55% body language.

Communication is more about how we speak than what we have to say. Getting to Yes, the original book on principled negotiation, talks about separating the people from the problem. In reality we need to separate the feelings from the problem.

Meeting Types and Timeframes

Meeting length and frequency also have a great affect on the outcome. It is not realistic to think that a problem can be presented, discussed and decided upon at a single meeting. The best decisions come from multiple meetings. Both the Quakers and Future Search use a three meeting process to introduce, discuss and decide on a course of action. Future Search maintains that two periods of sleep are needed to assimilate change. The Quakers require that an individual attend the first two meetings to be involved in the decision. We would do well to consider the wisdom of these groups.

Unified decision making has no tolerance of individual gain or glory. Instead, virtues, principles and reciprocity are all factors in the ultimate outcome which has the best interests of the community at heart. In summary, for the most effective communication, we need to use sight, sound and movement, and address both right and left-brain modes to understand and be understood by everyone.

Key #1 - Engage

This matter should be forcibly stressed by thee, so that consultation may be observed by all. (CONS, 93)

PRACTICES

Dynamic Consultation	Facilitative Mediation	World Cafe	Appreciative Inquiry	6 Hats
Engage	Ground Rules	Context Space		Blue

Facilitative Mediation - Ground rules - Allows the parties to set their own rules. Rules should be simple, fair and positive.

World Cafe - Set the Context - The parties should pay attention to the reason they are together, and what they want to achieve.

World Cafe - Create Hospitable Space - When people feel comfortable to be themselves, they do their most creative thinking, speaking, and listening.

Agreements for a Great Conversation: World Cafe
- Open-mindedness: listen to and respect all points of view
- Acceptance: suspend judgment as best you can
- Curiosity: seek to understand rather than persuade
- Discovery: question old assumptions, look for new insights
- Sincerity: speak for yourself about what has personal meaning
- Brevity: go for honesty and depth but don't go on and on

6 Thinking Hats - Process (Blue) - Sets process guidelines but does not offer any recommendations for specific rules.

Quaker Meeting uses a spiritually based 3 meeting process to make decisions, where the first meeting introduces the idea, the second for discussion and the third for decision.

Future Search observes that it takes 2 periods of sleep to assimilate change. The ground rules include:

- state your views and ask genuine questions;
- share all relevant information;
- use specific examples;
- explain your reasoning and intent;
- test assumptions and inferences; and
- discuss undiscussable issues.

Open Space, has "Four Principles" and "One Law" that are typically quoted and briefly explained during the opening briefing of an Open Space meeting. These explanations describe rather than control the process of the meeting. The four principles are:

- Whoever comes is the right people.
- Whenever it starts is the right time.
- Whatever happens is the only thing that could have.
- When it's over, it's over.

  Owen explains his one "Law," called the Law of Two Feet or "The Law of Mobility," as follows:

  If at any time during our time together you find yourself in any situation where you are neither learning nor contributing, use your two feet, go someplace else.

Skilled Facilitator offers five core values for groups:

- transparency, curiosity, accountability, informed choice and compassion.

Robert's Rules of Order is the default process for many groups. Robert's says "parliamentary law is the best method yet devised to enable assemblies of any size, with due regard for every member's opinion, to arrive at the general will on the maximum number of questions of varying complexity in a minimum amount of time and under all kinds of internal climate ranging from total harmony to hardened or impassioned division of opinion."

[Robert's Rules of Order Newly Revised [RONR (11th ed.), Introduction, p. liii]

Such systems as "Robert's Rules of Order" have no authority in Bahá'í consultation. Each Assembly should agree on the details necessary for maintaining an orderly flow of consultation and should revise them as required,

(GLSA, 3.7)

Roberta's Rules of Order provides a less formal, more feminine, and flexible approach. It replaces formality with informality; strict rules with guidelines and agreements; parliamentary procedure with democratic principles and processes; language of the 1800s with that of today; military terminology with civilian terminology; one-size fits all with flexibility, by culture; a framework designed for English and European males with that for a pluralistic society; win-lose voting with win-win decisions; a decision between two choices with straw polls and multiple choices; highly controlled and constrained meetings with those that are relaxed; and complicated with simple. Finally, Roberta's Rules of Order replaces debate with dialog, and it puts the motion AFTER a discussion of the problem and its solution, where it belongs.

Skills

If you don't know where you are going, you might wind up someplace else.

Yogi Berra

9 Keys	9 Skills with Questions
Engage	Process - What process should we adopt? Behavior - What behaviors do we expect?

"The first condition is absolute love and harmony amongst the members of the assembly....The second condition is that the members of the assembly should unitedly elect a chairman and lay down guide-lines and by-laws for their meetings and discussions. The chairman should have charge of such rules and regulations and protect and enforce them; the other members should be submissive, and refrain from conversing on superfluous and extraneous matters.... They must then proceed with the utmost devotion, courtesy, dignity, care and moderation to express their views. (SWAB, 88)

In Consultation the Chair is responsible for: (GLSA, 3.6-7)

- *Consulting with secretary about agenda*
- *Calling the meeting to order*
- *Ensuring free and open discussion*
- *Clarifying decisions or motions*
- *Helping group work within agreed upon guidelines*
- *Calling for a vote when appropriate*

Note that in many group models the Chair does not have a vote or a voice. In Bahá'í consultation, the Chair participates equally as a member of the group in any voting process.

Process

Building trust in a group is most closely associated with using a fair process. The agreement to implement a set of guidelines/rules such as the above enables each participant to feel safe in the consultative environment. It removes the barriers to unity and takes personalities out of the mix.

Process concerns who will facilitate the group and what method is used. A facilitator is like the saying "Take only pictures and leave only footsteps." As we will see, a good facilitator is a person who will bring out the best in a group.

The first agreement for any group is to agree on the chair/facilitator. The Chair is someone who is part of the group, the facilitator is someone who is outside the group. Either person should serve at the pleasure of the group and should consider his or herself as a servant leader.

The process rules include how we will proceed, when, where and how often we will meet, what is our goal in meeting, what steps will we use.

A positive environment would include one that is well lit, open and relaxed. Food is always a great addition when discussing difficult issues.

A positive goal allows for the possibility of a solution. See Key # 4, Envision, for a way to say the goal in positive terms.

Behavior

Behavior goals should include positive expectations like respect, openness and good faith. Guidelines should never be stated as negatives, e.g. no interrupting, no name calling.

Some possible guidelines might include:

- Speaking openly and honestly, Be humble and detached
- Listen actively and attentively, Respect other views,

- Detach from any preconceived notions,
- Fully and honestly disclose what we need to know
- Consider the views of others first
- Focus on first hand knowledge
- Willingly accept a better idea
- Everyone can speak once before anyone speaks again
- Regular periods of silence and reflection
- People learn at different rates and in different ways
- 2 periods of sleep for important decisions
- Consensus is preferred, but a may vote may be taken.
- See the evaluation section for a complete discussion.

What types of guidelines and by-laws do you think are the most helpful?

Case Story - The Right Side of the Tracks, Part II

What happened when 250 concerned citizens wanted to express their concern? What guidelines would you choose for public meeting like this?

Guidelines are the starting point for any consultation. Simple guidelines are the strongest.

The Guidelines

We set up a simple set of guidelines for our discussion.

1. Speak openly and honestly

2. Listen actively and attentively

3. Respect each other's point of view

4. Let everyone speak once before anyone speaks a second time

5. Offer constructive input

Divide and Conquer: the Constructive Way

Before the meeting, I had tentatively divided the topic areas into 9 different subject areas. I began by clarifying the topics and then we took a quick vote to prioritize them. We began with the topic of most interest. Anyone was allowed to ask a question or make a statement, either in person or written on a card.

Guideline #4 was the most interesting one. Many people wanted to speak and if a speaker had spoken once they automatically went to the end of the line, including elected officials who wanted to speak. This one rule gave the meeting a sense of fairness and greatly calmed everyone down.

All the questions were discussed and then consolidated to give to the city planners, which, in turn considered the questions, comments and concerns when drafting their final plan. The forum served its purpose of clarifying the concerns for inclusion into the final plan.

The project was actually completed on time and under budget. The tracks went underground and an open plaza area was created over them for community recreation. Though some still opposed the moving of history, most agreed that the tradeoffs of having fewer traffic delays, less noise pollution and greater safety made up for it. The City Public Works director won the national annual award for the project.

When there is an atmosphere of openness, honesty and trust, people are much more willing to participate in a constructive way.

Remember!

For a group to take ownership of the outcome, they need to begin by selecting a facilitator and creating their own guidelines, they need to create guidelines that are transparent, that promote a free exchange, that allow for silent reflection and that have the flexibility to be changed if needed.

EMPATHIZE

Key	Goal	Move from	To
Empathize	Feeling and Connecting	Talking	Listening

During the discussion, participants should make every effort to be frank and loving, candid and compassionate, while being actively interested in the views of others. Interaction should avoid conflict and contention. Emotional rapport should be built through positive questions and heartfelt responses. The facts and feelings together make up the total reality. This balance (empathy) between our perspective and another's is vital in growing our understanding and creating unity.

Bahá'í Writings

They must in every matter search out the truth and not insist upon their own opinion, for stubbornness and persistence in one's views will lead ultimately to discord and wrangling and the truth will remain hidden. (SWAB p. 88)

By God! Should one who is in affliction or grief read this Tablet with absolute sincerity, God will dispel his sadness, solve his difficulties and remove his afflictions. (Tablet of Ahmad)

Because the Most Great Peace is the object of our longing, a primary effort of the Bahá'í community is to reduce the incidence of conflict and contention, which have categorically been forbidden in the Most Holy Book. Does this mean that one may not express critical thought? Absolutely not. How can there be the candour called for in consultation if there is no critical thought? How is the individual to exercise his responsibilities to the Cause, if he is not allowed the freedom to express his views? Has Shoghi Effendi not stated that "at the very root of the Cause lies the principle of the undoubted right of the individual to self-expression, his freedom to declare his conscience and set forth his views"? (IRF, pp. 31-32)

When you notice that a stage has been reached when enmity and threats are about to occur, you should immediately postpone discussion of the subject, until wranglings, disputations, and loud talk vanish, and a propitious time is at hand. ('Abdu'l-Bahá, LOG, p. 178)

However, if we spontaneously desire to acknowledge we have been wrong in something, or that we have some fault of character, and ask another person's forgiveness or pardon, we are quite free to do so. The Guardian wants to point out, however, that we are not obliged to do so. It rests entirely with the individual. (CONS, pp. 12-13)

Please God, that we avoid the land of denial, and advance into the ocean of acceptance, so that we may perceive, with an eye purged from all conflicting elements, the worlds of unity and diversity, of variation and oneness, of limitation and detachment, and wing our flight unto the highest and innermost sanctuary of the inner meaning of the Word of God. (KI, p. 60)

So intense must be the spirit of love and loving kindness, that the stranger may find himself a friend, the enemy a true brother, no difference whatsoever existing between them. For universality is of God and all limitations earthly. Thus man must strive that his reality may manifest virtues and perfections, the light whereof may shine upon everyone. (WT, p. 13)

In all these thou shouldst find these binding relationships securely established. The more this inter-relationship is strengthened and expanded, the more will human society advance in progress and prosperity. Indeed without these vital ties it would be wholly impossible for the world of humanity to attain true felicity and success. (HQ, pp. 509-510)

This can be attained when every member expresseth with absolute freedom his own opinion and setteth forth his argument. Should anyone oppose, he must on no account feel hurt for not until matters are fully discussed can the right way be revealed. (SWAB, p. 87)

We return to the phenomenal characteristics of speech. Content, volume, style, tact, wisdom, timeliness are among the critical factors in determining the effects of speech for good or evil. Consequently, the friends need ever to be conscious of the significance of this activity which so distinguishes human beings from other forms of life, and they must exercise it judiciously. Their efforts at such discipline will give birth to an etiquette of expression worthy of the approaching maturity of the human race. Just as this discipline applies to the spoken word, it applies equally to the written word; and it profoundly affects the operation of the press. (IRF, p. 37)

We can never exert the influence over others which we can exert over ourselves. If we are better, if we show love, patience, and understanding of the weakness of others, if we seek to never criticize but rather encourage, others will do likewise. (LOG, 83)

They must then proceed with the utmost devotion, courtesy, dignity, care and moderation to express their views. (SWAB p. 88)

The Bahá'í Writings tell us that:

- We should begin by dispelling sadness.
- When emotions are high postpone the discussion.
- We may apologize but are not required to do so.
- We should first consider the views of others before advancing our own views.
- If we find an opinion that is more true and worthy we should accept it immediately.
- Everyone needs to be encouraged to express him/herself.
- We need to see unity in diversity
- Binding relationships help society prosper
- We need to see all perspectives to find the right path
- Show patience, love, understanding and encouragement.

Case Story - Native American Education, Part I

The local Indian tribal colony had its own education department and it was facing many challenges. Parents and staff were becoming very upset with the services and wanted to see change. They planned to hold a meeting to address all these problems and I was asked to facilitate the meeting.

People often see change as crisis (conflict) instead of insight (opportunity). Focusing on the conflict is like focusing on the dark, both are caused by the absence of light. You have to begin by focusing on what works and looking to the future. Stopping what isn't working isn't the same as starting what should be working. In the same way you focus on the virtues and not on the vices.

How would you promote empathy among 30 people who were in conflict with one another? How can you break the patterns of a broken past?

Feeling and Connecting

Our greatest freedom is the freedom to choose our attitude. — Victor Frankl

We attach an emotion to every situation we experience, and the emotion we feel is our choice. This reality is at the core of a field of human psychology that's come to be known as Emotional Intelligence (EI). Abdul Baha enforces this when He says " I will no longer be sorrowful. I will be a happy and joyful being."

Study of the concept of emotional (as opposed to analytical) intelligence dates from at least the 1940's and is a result of Darwin's early work on the importance of emotional expression to survival. EI found its application in the field of business management and human resources, and was popularized by Daniel Goleman's bestseller Emotional Intelligence: Why It Can Matter More Than IQ.

There are a number of variants on EI current in the psychological community, but the basic theory operates on the premise that though most of us accept feelings as being imposed upon us and believe that we have no choice about how we feel, the reality is otherwise. At the turn of the last century, William James said that, "The greatest discovery of my generation is that a human being can alter his or her life by altering his or her attitudes of mind."

This literally means that changing our feelings about a situation will allow us to think differently about it.

Emotion is what gives life meaning. Without emotion the world is a cold and lonely place. With too much emotion, life is overwhelming. Emotional Intelligence tells us that we naturally attach feelings to any situation we face. The situation and the feelings together give any event meaning for us, and it is that meaning that allows us to act. Emotions give life meaning and without emotion we would be paralyzed

As Stephen Covey writes: "Between stimulus and response is a choice" and that choice is how we feel. Emotion is what allows us to see the differences in things. Without emotion everything would look the same.

Negative Feelings

Life is a comedy for those who think and a tragedy for those who feel. — Noel Coward

Bad feelings and negative thoughts come from the material world. 'Abdu'l-Bahá said: "If we suffer, it is the outcome of material things..." (PT, p. 110.) These bad feelings are changed through spiritual activity. When we are in difficult situations, we are told to pray or to reflect on our personal circumstances. We feel better because we are calling on the spiritual world, which can bestow only joy.

Emotional Intelligence theory tells us when people are feeling down and out-of-touch with their spiritual selves, they have a set of negative thoughts that come to mind more readily. These bad thoughts bring on bad moods (EI, p. 73).

Since we attach an emotion to every experience or observation, our emotions drive our actions. We do what we feel. With positive emotions we can bring about a unified and peaceful future human civilization. With negative emotions, we can do untold damage. These positive feelings allow groups to perform at the highest level.

Skilled Facilitator says that "The single most important factor in maximizing the excellence of a group's product was the degree to which the members were able to create a state of internal harmony, which lets them take advantage of the full talent of their members (Schwarz, p. 67)."

When Bahá'ís are asked to weigh opinions with calmness, serenity and composure and to love each other in the spirit of fellowship, all of these attributes are reinforced. So we can see the importance of refraining from negative emotion.

Most modern group processes say that both positive and negative emotions are acceptable as part of the process. Emotional Intelligence uses the term "emotional hijacking" when parties take control through emotional outbursts. Bahá'ís, however, are given very explicit guidelines for the individual and the group to ensure the stability of the society. We will explore them further as this chapter unfolds.

How are feelings related to empathy?

O what a gift the gods they give us, to see ourselves as others see us. — Robert Burns

Empathy is one form of social exchange and most of Dynamic Consultation is based on this exchange theory. Empathy is our connection to each other, through both our perceptions and feelings. It is how well we understand the other's point of view and our emotional attachment to the situation. Trust is the principal ingredient of social exchange, where a current transaction becomes a future obligation.

Trust is built through risk, which is social exchange, where the parties act outside of each other's control, and must be trusted to "do right" by each other. Our decision-making capacity is most directly disrupted through negative thoughts (EI, p. 4). With negative thoughts we can't think clearly or creatively. Finally, unresolved issues of negative emotion limit our ability to function together (SF, p. 195).

Time can be our biggest enemy or our greatest ally when we are in a bad mood. During states of high agitation it takes us fifteen to thirty minutes just for the chemicals in our body to dissipate. We all know that when a child is agitated it's helpful to ask him/her to sit quietly until they calm down — the same applies to adults. Taking a time out to calm down can be the best medicine.

Positive Feelings

The best and most beautiful things in the world cannot be seen, nor touched ... but are felt in the heart. — Helen Keller

Bahá'í consultation offers a model of interaction that addresses the intellectual and spiritual parts of our reality. The two columns below show some of the attributes of consultation. Notice how the emotional attributes are all positive. None of them say that it is okay to vent to get it out of your system. Consultation and recent studies show that venting only harms people with words that cannot be readily taken back. Ideally we would adopt the qualities listed in each column. We would strive to be frank and loving, straightforward and compassionate, truthful and humble.

The following "Two Wings" of rationality and emotion are used in the Writings to describe consultation.

Rational	Emotional
Frank	Loving
Straightforwardness	Compassionate
Truthfulness	Humility
Overlook faults	Calmness
Honesty	Serenity
Trustworthiness	Composure
Unfettered	Amity
Understanding	Concord
Candor	Patience
Tact	Sincere kindliness
Wisdom	Fellowship
Devotion	Friendliness
Dignity	Unalloyed love
Moderation	Courtesy

Bahá'ís collapse the dichotomy of the rational and emotional sides of consultation into a single point of unity.

Emotional Intelligence tells us that our thoughts are associated with content and mood (EI, p. 73). We give meaning to any situation by the feelings we attach to it. However, if those feelings are choices, we need to reflect on how we feel about a difficult situation and see if we can decide to feel better about it.

The author does an exercise with his classes where he gives them a situation and ask them to write an "I" statement about it. An "I" statement says I feel _____ when _____ because _____. Therefore I would like to ask _____.

For example, a participant might write: I feel <u>humiliated</u> when <u>my boss disagrees with a point I've just made in a meeting,</u> because <u>I think it makes me look stupid or unprepared.</u> Therefore I would like to ask <u>that my boss be more sensitive to my feelings.</u>

After they write the first statement I ask them to deliberately decide to feel better about the situation and write a second statement. The feeling in the second statement always leads them to a better outcome.

For example, in the situation above, I might encourage the party to focus on the point his boss was making and what it tells him about how his boss views the issue, rather than on the effect it has had on his feelings.

A second statement written after some reflection might look like this: I feel <u>energized</u> when <u>my boss responds to a point I've just made</u> because <u>it means I've given him food for thought.</u> Therefore I would like to ask that <u>he tell me what he liked about my idea and what he didn't like about it so that I can get a better sense of his thought process.</u>

We also know that good moods enhance the ability to think flexibly and with more complexity (EI, p. 85). If we decide to feel better, we will be able to act better. People in good moods are more expansive and positive in their thinking. (EI, p. 85.)

How do we empathize?

People don't care how much you know until they know how much you care. - Theodore Roosevelt

Empathy is the caring aspect of ethics. Empathy is our connection to the perceptions and feelings of others. It is how well we understand their point of view and their emotional attachment.

In his book Emotional Intelligence, Goleman tells us that this emotional entrainment is the heart of influence (p. 117), that we influence others through our feelings. When our moods align we build rapport (p. 117); our physical attunement allows our moods to align. So literally mirroring another's actions will help build rapport. In Social Intelligence, his companion volume to EI, Goleman reports on brain research that concludes that an action by one person causes the same areas of the brain in the observing person to fire. Observation alone can build rapport through brain response.

The last question above is aimed at determining whether you must deal with your problems in the heat of the moment or have the "luxury" of waiting until these emotions have waned.

Conversely, physical attunement allows moods to align and, as previously noted, the coordination of moods is the essence of rapport. Emotional entrainment is the heart of influence and good moods enhance the ability to think flexibly and with more complexity. A sense of humor helps find a creative solution and people in good moods are more expansive and positive in their thinking.

In conclusion, empathy begins by listening to others. We need to consider the facts and feelings from multiple perspectives. We can then engage in meaningful dialogue filled with honesty and compassion.

In the key skill below, you'll see how empathy is encouraged in each of the techniques we've been discussing. Following the chart, you'll find practical advice about how to use empathy as a tool in your consultations.

Key #2 - Empathize

It is incumbent upon everyone to show the utmost love, rectitude of conduct, straightforwardness and sincere kindliness unto all the peoples and kindreds of the world, be they friends or strangers. (WT, 13)

PRACTICES

Dynamic Consultation	Facilitative Mediation	World Cafe	Appreciative Inquiry	6 Hats
Empathize	Questions	Questions	Discover	Red

Facilitative Mediation - Questions - allowing parties to feel what each is saying through questions.

World Cafe - Explore Questions that Matter - Knowledge emerges in response to compelling questions.

Appreciative Inquiry - DISCOVER - People work in pairs to tell stories of their past and current exceptional experiences about the topic of the inquiry.

6 Thinking Hats Emotions (Red) - Asks parties for their intuitive or instinctive gut reactions or statements of emotional feeling without justification, just "How do you feel about this?"

Transformative Mediation focuses on empathy and understanding through recognition and empowerment.

Skills

The first duty of love is to listen - Paul Tillich

9 Keys	9 Skills with Questions
Empathize	Listening - How can we listen first? Caring - How can we respond with love?

Empathy focuses on the heart using two key skills: listening and asking caring questions.

Listening

Listen positively with your whole being. Remember, body language is 55% of your communication. Face the person and don't be distracted. Remember the opposite of listening is preparing to speak.

Sit in silence - Don't be afraid of silence, we can only be in touch with our spirit when we are not physically engaged. (yes, silence is a skill). Let the silence be broken naturally.

Asking Caring Questions

Speak positively from your heart. Reflect on what is being said without offering advice or solutions.

Ask Positive questions that promote understanding. Try to understand the underlying feelings and reasons for the concerns.

It is vital to understand the feelings involved in any situation and the meaning behind those feelings. As always, the best way to achieve this understanding is to ask open, balanced, positive questions such as:

- How do you feel about the situation?

- How do others feel about it? Are they anxious, angry? How strong are the feelings?

- What is behind their feelings?

- Is the issue behind the feelings being addressed?

- What feelings do you share with the other parties?

- Common feelings could be the starting point for discussion. What feelings are different?

- How do you feel about resolving the issue?

- Is it important to resolve the issue now?

- Please tell me what happened.

- Can you give me an example?

- How are you feeling about this?

- Can you tell me more about the situation?

- What did you mean when you said...?

- Can you explain more about...?

- Why do you think that happened?

- Why do others believe there is a problem?

- It sounds as if we have very different perceptions of what happened.

- Has anything like this happened before?

- What is the worst part of the problem?

- What is most important to you about this problem?

Case Story - Native American Education, Part II

How was empathy promoted? I had everyone sit in a circle and we began the day with a native blessing focusing on the virtues of the community. The purpose of the prayer was to remind those present to allow the common virtues of unity, humility and trust to manifest in our discussion. I then asked everyone to take out a piece of paper and write down his or her one best idea for the education department. Once they had done that I asked them to pass the paper to the person on their right. I then asked everyone to accept the gift they had been given and add to it to make it a better idea. We continued to add to each idea six more times so each idea had been through "Seven generations," a significant native concept.

I then asked everyone to post their idea on the wall and to group similar ideas together. I asked everyone to look at the ideas and if you had another you wanted to include you could add it to the ones up there. We named each group of ideas. We then did a quick priority vote to determine which group we would work on first. You always want to start on the area where there is the most interest because otherwise people will be distracted until their issue is discussed.

In less than 30 minutes from when we started we had 30 refined ideas, grouped and prioritized. We then started working together on the future, developing the ideas into meaningful action. All of our work began with a common set of virtues guiding our interaction.

Remember! To help someone using sympathy, get out of the lifeboat and into the water. To help someone with empathy, help them into the lifeboat. Empathy begins with caring, leads to healing and builds solid relationships. Once you dispel the sadness you can begin to solve the difficulty and remove the affliction.

EXPLORE

Key	Goal	Move from	To
Explore	Learning and Knowing	Conjecture	Certainty

Information should be gathered from a wide range of sources, with diverse points of view represented. Speak honestly from your own understanding and listen with an open heart and an open mind. Understand the facts of the situation and explore the reasons behind the actions. This is done by asking open, positive questions that promote positive answers.

Bahá'í Writings

Consultation bestoweth greater awareness and transmuteth conjecture into certitude. It is a shining light which, in a dark world, leadeth the way and guideth. For everything there is and will continue to be a station of perfection and maturity. The maturity of the gift of understanding is made manifest through consultation. (CC, I, 93)

When the human soul soareth out of this transient heap of dust and riseth into the world of God, then veils will fall away, and verities will come to light, and all things unknown before will be made clear, and hidden truths be understood. (SWAB, 177)

Investigation of Reality

There are only four accepted methods of comprehension—that is to say, the realities of things are understood by these four methods.

The first method is by the senses—that is to say, all that the eye, the ear, the taste, the smell, the touch perceive is understood by this method. Today this method is considered the most perfect by all the European philosophers: they say that the principal method of gaining knowledge is through the senses; they consider it supreme, although it is imperfect, for it commits errors. For example, the greatest of the senses is the power of sight. The sight sees the mirage as water, and it sees images reflected in mirrors as real and existent; large bodies which are distant appear to be small, and a whirling point appears as a circle. The sight believes the earth to be motionless and sees the sun in motion, and in many similar cases it makes mistakes. Therefore, we cannot trust it.

The second is the method of reason, which was that of the ancient philosophers, the pillars of wisdom; this is the method of the understanding. They proved things by reason and held firmly to logical proofs; all their arguments are arguments of reason. Notwithstanding this, they differed greatly, and their opinions were contradictory. They even changed their views—that is to say, during twenty years they would prove the existence of a thing by logical arguments, and afterward they would deny it by logical arguments—so much so that Plato at first logically [298] proved the immobility of the earth and the movement of the sun; later by logical arguments he proved that the sun was the stationary center, and that the earth was moving. Afterward the Ptolemaic theory was spread abroad, and the idea of Plato was entirely forgotten, until at last a new observer again called it to life. Thus all the mathematicians disagreed, although they relied upon arguments of reason. In the same way, by logical arguments, they would prove a problem at a certain time, then afterward by arguments of the same nature they would deny it. So one of the philosophers would firmly uphold a theory for a time with strong arguments and proofs to support it, which afterward he would retract and contradict by arguments of reason. Therefore, it is evident that the method of reason is not perfect, for the differences of the ancient philosophers, the want of stability and the variations of their opinions, prove this. For if it were perfect, all ought to be united in their ideas and agreed in their opinions.

The third method of understanding is by tradition—that is, through the text of the Holy Scriptures—for people say, "In the Old and New Testaments, God spoke thus." This method equally is not perfect, because the traditions are understood by the reason. As the reason itself is liable to err, how can it be said that in interpreting the meaning of the traditions it will not err, for it is possible for it to make mistakes, and certainty cannot be attained. This is the method of the religious leaders; whatever they understand and comprehend from the text of the books is that which their reason understands from the text, and not necessarily the real truth; for the reason is like a balance, and the meanings contained in the text of the Holy Books are like the thing which is weighed. If the balance is untrue, how can the weight be ascertained?

Know then: that which is in the hands of people, that which they believe, is liable to error. For, in proving or disproving a thing, if a proof is brought forward which is taken from the evidence of our senses, this method, as has become evident, is not perfect; if the proofs are intellectual, the same is true; or if they are traditional, such proofs also are not perfect. Therefore, there is no standard in the hands of people upon which we can rely.

But the bounty of the Holy Spirit gives the true method of comprehension which is infallible and indubitable. This is through the help of the Holy Spirit which comes to man, and this is the condition in which certainty can alone be attained. (SAQ, 83)

Consultation is about probing deeper into our understanding of any situation. As we investigate reality we need to understand the tools at our disposal. We know that the Holy Spirit is the unerring way to truth but how can we access the bounty of the Holy Spirit? To do this we have five outer powers and four spiritual powers.

Physical and Spiritual Powers

In man five outer powers exist, which are the agents of perception—that is to say, through these five powers man perceives material beings. These are sight, which perceives visible forms; hearing, which perceives audible sounds; smell, which perceives odors; taste, which perceives foods; and feeling, which is in all parts of the body and perceives tangible things. These five powers perceive outward existences.

Man has also spiritual powers: imagination, which conceives things; thought, which reflects upon realities; comprehension, which comprehends realities; memory, which retains whatever man imagines, thinks and comprehends. The intermediary between the five outward powers and the inward powers is the sense which they possess in common—that is to say, the sense which acts between the outer and inner powers, conveys to the inward powers whatever the outer powers discern. It is termed the common faculty, because it communicates between the outward and inward powers and thus is common to the outward and inward powers. (SAQ, page 211)

Scientific knowledge is the highest attainment upon the human plane, for science is the discoverer of realities. It is of two kinds: material and spiritual. [924] Material science is the investigation of natural phenomena; divine science is the discovery and realization of spiritual verities. The world of humanity must acquire both. A bird has two wings; it cannot fly with one. Material and spiritual science are the two wings of human uplift and attainment. Both are necessary—one the natural, the other supernatural; one material, the other divine. By the divine we mean the discovery of the mysteries of God, the comprehension of spiritual realities, the wisdom of God, inner significances of the heavenly religions and foundation of the law. (PUP, p. 924)

Our purpose of life is to be a good person and to do kind acts. If this is what we are striving for, what guidance would we choose? What fruit would you choose to grow? Is a tree in the orchard without fruit worth maintaining? Is a life without purpose worth living?

While we do know we have these powers, we don't know the capacity, duration appearance or properties of these powers. To say they exist doesn't advance our understanding. If these powers and capacities exist, but are hidden, what clues could we look for? We know that they connect to physical reality at some point. What and where are these connections?

Consultation is the path toward developing a deeper understanding of physical reality and the connection between the physical and the spiritual.

In conclusion, the Bahá'í Writings tell us that:

- Holy Spirit is the true method of understanding.
- We can see and recognize truth with our spiritual powers.
- Truth enables progress and leads to unity.
- Accessing our spirit allows truth to come to light.
- Truth is known through the heart.
- Truth is known through individual investigation.
- Truth is saying what is seen and unseen.
- Truth is rational investigation, confirmed by actual experience.
- Truth comes forth after the clash of differing opinions.
- Truth expressed with enthusiasm and vigor, not from clash of feelings.
- Truth develops trust and creates points of unity.
- Truth the best understanding a group can reach.

Case Story - High School at Lunch, Part I

High school students at an at-risk school were getting into trouble during lunch time off campus. They were late for class and some of them did not return after lunch. The teachers and parents were very upset and wanted action taken.

I was asked to help them resolve the issue. The campus had faced many challenges with high school kids leaving over lunch and acting irresponsibly while off-campus. Conversely, there were many difficulties in having them stay on campus over lunch, so we wanted to have a discussion around making the best decision for all concerned.

We asked about eighty teachers, parents and students to come together and discuss this.

What could the students, parents and teachers learn from each other? How would the students respond? What would the parents and teachers do?

Learning and Knowing

The only difference between a problem and a solution is that people understand the solution.

Charles Kettering

Our perspective is the way we view reality. It's the combination of how we take in the world around us and what we think about it. When we interact with others, we are using our filter of the world and they are using their filter of the world. Filters include the four mentioned in the quote above: senses, reason, tradition and the Holy Spirit. It's this reconciliation of different worldviews that becomes our first challenge in making difficult decisions. As mentioned before, through processing and perceiving we develop an understanding of the world around us. Next we compare our understanding of the world with other perspectives.

When we come across a new situation, some of us sense and feel our way, while others think things through to connect the experience to rational meaning. The primary way of acquiring knowledge and certitude proposed by 'Abdu'l-Bahá is with the help of the Holy Spirit. Through it, we can see that we are both one and apart, with inherent differences and similarities, but each has spiritual capacity.

A number of researchers have identified similar paths in the ways that we learn. Their research has yielded a number of variants on learning models. One of the models that combines several different paths is called 4MAT.

4MAT takes research from eight different models of learning and combines those into a single model. It begins with the work of Carl Jung and ends most recently with David Kolb. All the work from these researchers has resulted in a visual diagram of learning styles that places each of four learning methods in a quadrant of the diagram.

The 4MAT process identifies two spectrums:

How people perceive the world around them

How they process what they perceive

Diagram of 4MAT

Sensing/Feeling

Implication		**Connection**
What if? - 4		1 - Why?
Active		Reflective
How? - 3		2 - What?
Application		**Examination**

Thinking

Perceiving — Active to Reflective

Processing—Sensing/Feeling to Thinking

The 4MAT process identifies two spectrums:

· How people perceive the world around them

· How they process what they perceive

The spectrum around perception has to do with sensing and feeling at one end and thinking at the other. The spectrum around processing has active experimentation at one end and reflective observation at the other. When we combine these two spectrums, we come up with four quadrants as you can see from the diagram.

The 4MAT diagram encourages us to value people whose learning modality falls in any quadrant, recognizing that this form of diversity contributes greatly to our growth as a society.

The differences in the way people learn depend on many things: who we are, where we are, how we see ourselves and what people ask of us. However, there are two major differences in how we learn. The first is how we perceive the world around us, how we take in that world and how we interact with that world. Perceiving ranges from active experimentation to reflective observation. The second major difference is how we process the world around us, how we think and feel about that world, how we make it part of ourselves.

As we perceive the world around us some of us jump right in and try it, while others watch what is happening and reflect on it. If we jump right in and try it, we are called active learners. If we stand back and watch the world, we are called reflective learners. The observers tend to reflect on new things and filter these new things through their own experience to create meaningful connections. The doers act on new information immediately. They reflect once they have tried it out and extended it into their world.

Only when we combine these two modalities in context with virtue and a principle-based decision-making process can we truly make ethical decisions.

If we consider the learning characteristics from the four quadrants illustrated above, we come up with some interesting observations.

· In the first quadrant are the imaginative learners. They perceive information concretely, and process it reflectively. They integrate experience with the self, they learn by listening and sharing ideas. They work in harmony, and they need to be personally involved.

· Analytic learners in the second quadrant perceive information abstractly and process it reflectively. They devise theories by integrating their observations into what is known. They seek continuity; they need to know what the experts think. They learn by thinking through ideas.

· In quadrant three, are the commonsense learners. They perceive information abstractly and process it actively. They integrate theory and practice. They learn by testing theories and applying common sense. They are pragmatists and they believe that if it works, they should use it.

· In the fourth quadrant are dynamic learners, who perceive information concretely and process it actively. They integrate experience in application and learn by trial and error. They're adaptable and even relish change, and they often reach accurate conclusions in the absence of logical justification.

How we perceive and how we process information forms our own learning style. This combination is different for all; each one of us has unique capacities and abilities tied to our physical being. Most of us don't fit neatly into one category, but have aspects of all four in greater or lesser strength.

The first step in any difficult situation, therefore, is reconciling the different perspectives that people bring to the situation. We need to recognize the unique contributions that each of those four quadrants can provide and to work with all four of them. When we can use all four learning styles, we are connecting with everyone. We need to feel comfortable in, and seek participation from, each of those quadrants, because each learning modality offers unique gifts to any situation.

It's when we can get all four modalities to work together that we truly have unity in diversity. Ethical challenges often occur because people fail to consider that others might perceive things differently.

Communication through consultation is essential to seeing things through another's eyes and resolving disputes. People use their own frame of reference and tend to jump to conclusions about others' motivations.

What is Perspective?

Every man takes the limits of his own field of vision for the limits of the world. — Arthur Schopenhauer

Our life is going along smoothly, then something unexpected happens and a problem needs to be solved. If it becomes an emotional issue, it could turn into conflict. In any situation like this, we begin with our own understanding of the situation.

Facts are objective information based on our sensory perception. In any situation, we begin by understanding how we perceive the world around us. Next, we associate feelings with the facts. Our brain does this automatically. These feelings drive our actions. Finally, framing a situation allows us to look at the facts from broader and different perspectives. All three together provide a complete model for understanding a situation.

The starting point in problem-solving is considering all the perspectives in any situation. In the past, problem solving concerned the theory of "what's in it for me?" Each person involved in the problem had a vested interest to solve the problem his way. This vested interest did not concern itself with our interconnectedness. In more recent times, however the modern theory of group process is starting to recognize the role full consideration plays in helping groups work together.

Determining the facts requires asking questions. The following fact-finding steps all center on specific questions to ask to find out as much as possible about any situation.

Determine the nature and dimensions of the dilemma. There are several avenues you can take to ensure that you have examined the problem in all its various dimensions. Try to see the issue through the eyes of the community. In practice, this translates into understanding local principles, which are valued and respected, such as religious tenets and established customs. For Bahá'ís, of course, moral choices need to be weighed in light of the guidance found in the Bahá'í Writings.

Regardless of these variances, the goal is to consider the matter based on what the community believes is right. Often there is no clear-cut "right" choice; instead, there are dozens of viable options. More choices usually mean better decisions. We must weigh these options considering their possible consequences and decide which option promotes the virtues and principles that are identified as valuable and causes the least amount of harm to all involved.

According to the Bahá'í Writings (indeed, according to all revealed scripture), our goal in life is to develop our spiritual capacities. Our virtues and principles allow us to do this. When murky questions of right and wrong arise, revisiting these fundamental teachings will help guide us to thoughtful decisions. The Bahá'í Faith respects the right of every individual to pursue his or her dreams and goals using his/her particular talents. We can use the Bahá'í Writings to light our paths along the river of life and to act as a bumper to remind us of the boundaries within which we must steer.

Truth

God has given man the eye of investigation by which he may see and recognize truth. Each human creature has individual endowment, power and responsibility in the creative plan of God.
(PUP, 293)

Truthfulness is the foundation of all human virtues. Without truthfulness progress and success, in all the worlds of God, are impossible for any soul. When this holy attribute is established in man, all the divine qualities will also be acquired."

(ADJ, page 26)

Before expressing his own views he should carefully consider the views already advanced by others... Even a majority opinion or consensus may be incorrect. A thousand people may hold to one view and be mistaken, whereas one sagacious person may be right... If he finds that a previously expressed opinion is more true and worthy, he should accept it immediately and not willfully hold to an opinion of his own. (PUP, 72-73)

Consultation seeks to explore and understand the truth of a situation. Truth has come under fire over the last decade as a judgmental and outmoded concept, and one that purports to infringe on the rights of people. My truth is stronger than your truth is a common sentiment.

Truth is considered as a relative and inconsequential aspect in modern conflict resolution. However, real solutions need to be based on a clear, open and consistent understanding of the facts.

But what is truth? Is it what I know, what I believe or what I see? Is it objective or subjective? Is it relative or fixed? Let's consider truth from a number of different perspectives and show that truth is an indispensable part of our lives.

Truth begins as the foundation of Western Civilization, Aristotle based his philosophy on truth and reason. Buddha says there is my truth, your truth and the truth. The US Declaration of Independence says "We hold these truths to be self-evident, that all men are created equal, that they are endowed by their Creator with certain unalienable Rights, that among these are Life, Liberty and the pursuit of Happiness."

Truth is the foundation of our legal system. Witnesses in the US court system are asked to agree that they will tell the truth, the whole truth and nothing but the truth. Truth comes through openly sharing the perspectives of everyone involved. Solutions that are not based on the truth will not last long.

Truth has several questions to consider in consultation: Do we have complete knowledge (the whole truth)? Do we have correct knowledge (nothing but the truth)? Will the facts change over time (consistent truth)?

The first step in exploring a situation is to verify you have a complete understanding of the facts. Are there discrepancies or contradictions? You need to ask kind, honest questions to come a complete understanding.

Secondly, you need to make sure that you have a complete understanding. Are the other aspects we are missing? Have we heard from everyone with first hand knowledge?

Finally, have or will the facts change over time? Some situations change naturally and you make sure that the issue still exists.

The purpose of truthfulness is to build trust. Without truth, trust is absent and action is almost impossible. With truth you can start to build trust and take unified action. Truth is a vital component of consultation.

Key #3 Explore

The fact that we imagine ourselves to be right and everybody else wrong is the greatest of all obstacles in the path towards unity, and unity is necessary if we would reach truth, for truth is one.
(PT, 136)

Practices

Dynamic Consultation	Facilitative Mediation	World Cafe	Appreciative Inquiry	6 Hats
Explore	Storytelling Issues	Contributions		White

Facilitative Mediation - Storytelling - expressing the facts and identifying the issues in an open, honest and sincere way.

World Cafe - Encourage Everyone's Contribution - It is important to encourage everyone in your meeting to contribute their ideas and perspectives, while also allowing anyone who wants to participate by simply listening to do so.

6 Thinking Hats Information: (White) - considering purely what information is available, what are the facts?

Skills

**There is always a way to be honest without being brutal.
Arthur Dobrin**

9 Keys	9 Skills with Questions
Explore	Powers - How can we use our spirit and senses? Questions - How can we ask better questions?

Powers

Our powers are our physical senses. We need to be totally present in heart , mind and body. We have to be aware and alert , and positively focused. We need to separate fact from fiction, and not overly speculate.

Questions

Computers are useless, they can only give you answers.

Pablo Picasso

The only tool we have to explore reality is a good question.

Consider these steps in asking questions:

1) A person should first understand his/her own view of the situation clearly (which is not always as easy as it sounds).

Ask: What are the facts from my perspective?

2) Next, listen to firsthand knowledge from other parties.

Ask: What is their perspective? Listen to all perspectives with an eye to identifying the problem.

3) Gather as much information as you can to illuminate the situation. In doing so, it is important to be as specific and ob-jective as possible. Use firsthand sources from people that have direct knowledge of the situation. Consider the other parties' perspectives.

Ask: What do they know that will help illuminate the situation? How might they view the facts?

4) From all of these perspectives, identify the problem. Writing ideas down may help you gain clarity.

Ask: What is the issue as they see it?

5) Outline the facts, separating out innuendo, assumptions, hypotheses, or suspicions.

Ask: What are the objective facts of the situation?

6) **Ask** more questions. Other questions you might want to ask include:

Is the issue related to me and what I am or am not doing? Is it related to an institution or agency and its policies and procedures? (If the problem can be resolved by implementing one of the policies of an institution or agency, you can look to the agency's guidelines.)

The dilemmas you face are often complex — a complexity that's only increased by the number of possible perspectives. For that very reason, I recommend you avoid searching for a simplistic solution.

4MAT: Teaching to Learning Styles offers 4 questions for us to consider:

Quadrant 1	Ask, "Why?"
Quadrant 2	Ask, "What?"
Quadrant 3	Ask, "How?"
Quadrant 4	Ask, "What if?"

ASKING BETTER QUESTIONS

Neutral

|

1 | 2

Open _____ Closed

|

3 | 4

Positional

The key to promoting open, positive dialogue is asking questions. The horizontal line represents the spectrum from open to closed questions, the vertical line represents positional to neutral questions.

1) Positive Open, neutral questions ask for a narrative response. You are encouraging someone to tell you what they know and believe. You don't have a preconceived opinion and are merely looking for information.

2) Positive neutral questions are looking to verify what the speaker believes to be true.

3) Positive Open positional questions are asking the speaker to respond with their opinion or knowledge around what the questioner is assuming.

4) Positive Closed positional questions are only to verify what is accepted as true.

5) Better questions begin as open and neutral in quadrant 1.

As demonstrated below, an open-ended question may be more effective than a closed question:

Question: Why did you take his book? (Q3)

Question: How can we locate the missing book?(Q1)

Question: Did you start this fight? (Q4)

Question: Do you know who started this? (Q2)

Sample Q1 (Why?) questions:

· Has anything like this happened before? Why do others believe there is a problem?

· Please tell me what happened. Why do you think that happened?

· Can you tell me more about the situation? What do we think is really going on here?

Sample Q2 (What?) questions:

· Can you give me an example? Can you explain more about...?

· It sounds as if we have very different perceptions of what happened.

What is the worst part of the problem? What did you mean when you said...?

· What is the best solution for everyone? What is most important to you about this problem?

· What would it take for us to feel the problem has been solved?

Case Story - High School at Lunch, Part II

How does searching after truth promote a more positive outcome?

6 Thinking Hats (book by the same name) is a very effective model for group process that was developed by Dr. Edward DeBono, a brain researcher from Harvard University. DeBono maintains that groups can be more effective when they align their thinking. This is done by asking everyone the group to wear the same "hat" at the same time. This compartmentalization provides a very productive atmosphere for discussion.

There are only two rules with 6 Hats:

1.) Everyone agrees to wear the same hat at the same time and

2.) Only the facilitator (chair) can call for a change in hats. When everyone wears the same hat the group can proceed productively through deep and difficult issues.

Six Thinking Hats looks at:

- The issues we are facing,
- New ideas that will address those issues,
- Why they will work,
- Why they won't work,
- What information we need to know
- How we feel about the situation.

The parents and teachers began cautiously, unsure of what the students would demand and how they should respond.

Everyone identified all the reasons that an open campus would work and not work, and the reasons a closed campus would work and not work (the truth of the situation). When the parents and the teachers saw that the students recognized all the challenges that an open campus presented, they were willing to allow the students to have an open campus. The students were able to see the situation from the parents' and teachers' perspective, and the parents and teachers were able to see the situation from the student's perspective. (A fourth perspective in this case is that of the community, which would be affected by any student's misbehavior.)

Open Campus During Lunch

	Will work	Won't work
Parents	Responsibility	Absenteeism
Teachers	Positive behavior	Time crunch
Students	Food choices	Bad behavior

Considering this model, we can only take the correct actions when we feel they are the right thing to do. This feeling should come as the result of prayer and reflection. Moral issues lead to moral judgment, which leads to moral intent and ends in moral behavior.

When the parents and teachers saw that the students understood the truth of the situation, they were willing to allow them to have an open campus. In this case empathy plus honesty equals moral growth.

Remember!

Understand your perspective, Listen to others

Gather information, Ask questions that are neutral and open

Identify the problem, Outline the facts, Consult experts

All truths are easy to understand once they are discovered; the point is to discover them. — Galileo

ENVISION

Key	Goal	Move from	To
Envision	Framing and Focusing	Parts	Whole

Identify the greater purpose and vision for what you are trying to accomplish. Create a balanced, positive, future-focused frame. A frame is a broader statement of the problem that allows for a wider range of solutions.

Bahá'í Writings

It is not for him to pride himself who loveth his own country, but rather for him who loveth the whole world. The earth is but one country, and mankind its citizens. (TAB, p. 167)

Every imperfect soul is self-centered and thinketh only of his own good. But as his thoughts expand a little he will begin to think of the welfare and comfort of his family. If his ideas still more widen, his concern will be the felicity of his fellow citizens; and if still they widen, he will be thinking of the glory of his land and of his race. But when ideas and views reach the utmost degree of expansion and attain the stage of perfection, then will he be interested in the exaltation of humankind. He will then be the well-wisher of all men and the seeker of the weal and prosperity of all lands. This is indicative of perfection. (SWAB, 69)

In conclusion, the Bahá'í Writings tell us that:

- We need to love the whole world

- We need to let our ideas and views reach the utmost degree of expansion and attain the stage of perfection, then will we will be interested in the exaltation of humankind

- A single, universal perceptive power allows differing opinions to merge, so that a spiritual harmony and oneness will become apparent.

Case Story: Barking Dog, Part I

I was asked to come in and work with a group of homeowners in a case regarding a barking dog. This case involved about twenty people in the neighborhood.

I asked only four questions, but the way that I framed those questions opened up the possibilities for resolution. Here are the questions:

First set of questions: Where do you live? How long have you lived there? What are your hopes and dreams for the community?

Each person went up to a map, showed where they lived and how long they had been there, and what spoke about their hopes and dreams were for the community.

One person got up and said he and his spouse had lived there for five years and were looking forward to raising a family there.

Another couple got up and said that they had only lived there a few months and were just renting until they could afford a place.

The next person got up and said they had just sold their house and were leaving within the next few months.

Someone else got up and said they had been there about a year and were very happy with living there.

Thus, we began questions that allowed people to connect with one another.

The questions continued in like manner:

"What would you like to share about your dog?"

Everyone in the neighborhood had a dog and they all wanted to share what was important to them about the about the dog they owned.

"What is normal for a dog in your neighborhood?"

Someone said, "While it's okay if they come on my lawn, I don't want them on my front porch."

Someone else said, "Well, I guess they could come in my backyard occasionally."

Another said dogs should always be on a leash and that they should be quiet after 10:00 PM.

Finally: How should this issue be framed?

One more question framed the situation and resolved the issue. What was the question?

Framing and Focusing

The opening quote is a wonderful examples of progressively framing an issue. It begins with the individual, then family, next are citizens, followed by land and race, and ending with the exaltation of humankind. Framing an issue in terms of the exaltation of humankind places us in the realm of unity and will lead to amazing outcomes.

We all begin with only our own comfort and interests in mind, much like a baby when it is born. As the child grows, she becomes aware of her family. When she goes to school, she becomes aware of her fellow students and community. When she leaves school, she becomes aware of her nation. The final step in her maturation process is to become aware of the state of humankind. Only then will she be able to seek the weal and prosperity of all.

Framing is how you state the problem. A frame is a more expansive statement than the problem itself. The first step in resolving any issue is to frame it in a way that provides the opportunity for more creative and expansive solutions. Most situations start out framed with Yes or No solutions: If you're right, then I'm wrong. The key to resolution is expanding the understanding of the problem which will allow for a wider range of choices.

Why is framing important?

Framing is stating the problem in a way that encompasses all perspectives, is neutral, future-focused and allows for the possibility of a solution. Framing broadens the issue beyond the narrow positions of the parties and allows them a greater freedom to resolve the issue.

The initial starting point for any negotiation or decision is a position. People polarize into positions which narrowly express their views on resolving a given situation. At the beginning, self-interest or group interest in a larger context is the main focus. (How can I/we get what we want?—Think politics.)

Framing broadens the issue beyond the narrow positions of the parties and allows them a greater freedom to resolve the issue. Thinking of the earth as one country is one way to unify all the peoples of the world into one human family—a family that you care for and want to see prosper.

Framing allows us to generate a wider range of options and thus have more creative solutions. Brainstorming research has shown that the best predictor of a good outcome is having a greater number of choices available.

How can framing be used to increase choices?

We opened this section with a story about a barking dog. The frame was to promote neighborhood unity, the questions were around everyone working together to help a dog who wasn't able to live peacefully in the neighborhood.

Suggestions for developing a frame

· Listen first and listen to the minority.

· Consider each other's perspective.

· Develop a shared understanding.

· Break down a complex issue into component parts.

· Group activity of understanding - draw a picture of the situation, write a song around the problem

· Once everyone has a complete and shared understanding of the issues, the problem can be framed.

Key #4 - Envision

So long as the powers of the mind are various, it is certain that men's judgments and opinions will differ one from another. If, however, one single, universal perceptive power be introduced - a power encompassing all the rest - those differing opinions will merge, and a spiritual harmony and oneness will become apparent. (SWAB, 63)

Practices

Dynamic Consultation	Facilitative Mediation	World Cafe	Appreciative Inquiry	6 Hats
Envision	Frame	Define		

Facilitative Conflict Resolution - Framing - defining the issues collectively in future focused terms.

Appreciative Inquiry - DEFINE - the topic of inquiry from an AI perspective. "How would staff interact if all were being cooperative and treating each other like customers?"

A good frame is the "aha" moment, you know it when you say it. When you frame an issue well, you are on the downhill slope for resolving the issue.

Skills

The greatest challenge to any thinker is stating the problem in a way that will allow a solution.
Bertrand Russell

9 Keys	9 Skills with Questions
Envision	Vision - What is the big picture? Framing - How can we work together to ....?

Vision

Why is this issue important? What are the benefits of resolving this issue? Look at the issue outside of the local context. Ask what others would do to solve this issue.

Framing

Framing is an excellent way to generate a wide variety of choices around any issue. It is taking the "30,000 foot view" of the issue. A frame states the problem in a way that is:

• **Future focused**—look at the problem and the resolution from the perspective of the future. How would it feel to resolve the issue to everyone's satisfaction?

• **Neutral**—the problem should be stated in a way that does not favor one party over another. Don't blame one party. Offer everyone the opportunity to work together.

• **Looks at the big picture**—look beyond the narrow interests of the parties and look at the big picture.

• **Positive**—what is the positive change you want to move toward, not the negative change you want to move away from. In the dog example, it was asking, "What is normal for a dog in your neighborhood?" Approach the problem with positive intention, knowing that it can be solved in a way that will benefit everyone.

• **And allows for the possibility of a solution**—problems should have a range of acceptable solutions, so state the problem in a way that allows the positive solutions to become apparent.

Samples of Framing

There is no one best frame. Each of these shows a better frame than the initial one.

• <u>ISSUE</u>: One neighbor has a barking dog.

Initial frames: Your dog has to go! My dog has to stay!

Better frame: How can we work together to help your dog?

• <u>ISSUE</u> Tenants refuse to pay rent.

Initial frames: They need to be evicted. This apartment needs to be repaired.

Better frame: How can this apartment meet everyone's needs?

• <u>ISSUE</u> Business refuses to refund money for product.

Initial frames: I will sue them to get my money! They agreed to buy the product.

Better frame: How can we address the needs of both the business and the consumer?

- **ISSUE**: Employee evaluation

Initial frames: This employee doesn't work well. My boss doesn't care.

Better frame: What could be done to help all employees work at a higher level?

- **ISSUE** Teaching children's classes

Initial frame: Teaching children is very important, but it seems an impossible task. Today's children behave poorly and nobody can stand to be around them.

Better frame: Teaching children is important and something I like to do. The children in the village are very special and I consider them my friends.

Case Story: Barking Dog, Part II

What question would you ask? In this case I decided to frame the issue in terms of the neighborhood instead of a single individual. I also focused on the dog's perspective.

"How can we help a dog that can't live according to the norms of this neighborhood?"

Below is the set of questions as posted on the flip chart.

Four Questions

Where do you live?

What would you share about your dog?

What is normal for a dog in your neighborhood?

How can we help a dog that can't live according to the norms of this neighborhood?

The neighbors in the Case of the Barking Dog worked together and came up with a very creative list of about twenty different things that they could do to help a dog that couldn't live according to the community norms. We took that list and put it in order by cost, so we started with the least expensive and moved toward the most expensive.

The least expensive included things like install a doggie door (so the dog could go inside at will), put a radio outside the house for the dog, have the dog socialize with other dogs and people. The more expensive choices were things like doggie day care, doggie psychiatrists and doggie Valium. We did not end up with an agreement so much as we ended up with a prioritized list. It was agreed that the dog owner would start with the least expensive idea and just keep working down the list until he found the things that worked.

Prioritizing choices by cost

Allow the dog to socialize with other dogs

Allow the dog to socialize with neighbors

Place a radio in the background

Install a doggie door into the garage... +10 other ideas then,

Doggie valium

Doggie day care

Now, the interesting thing in this case was that I never found out who owned the dog that was misbehaving because that was not important. Nobody ever pointed a finger; nobody ever said "You did something wrong, dog owner." It was all about working together to solve the problem, sitting in a circle of equals around the list of issues and the proposed solutions which, in the spirit of consultation, belonged to everyone equally. When you take the global perspective, no one has to defend or be accused of wrongdoing.

Remember!

Frame the issue to generate more and better options!

Use positive, balanced, future focused terms.

Ask "How can we work together to...?

EXPAND

Key	Goal	Move from	To
Expand	Creativity and Options	Limited	Many

Create a diverse, positive and creative set of choices. Positive thinking helps create more choices and more choices leads to better decisions. Ideas presented become the property of the group rather than an individual or constituency. Lack of retained ownership allows for the free flow of discussion of an idea without anyone feeling defensive.

Bahá'í Quotes

The purpose of consultation is to show that the views of several individuals are assuredly preferable to one man, even as the power of a number of men is of course greater than the power of one man. (CONS, 97)

He who expresses an opinion should not voice it as correct and right but set it forth as a contribution to the consensus of opinion... (PUP, 72).

Some things are subject to the free will of man, such as justice, equity, tyranny and injustice, in other words, good and evil actions; it is evident and clear that these actions are, for the most part, left to the will of man... In all the action or inaction of man, he receives power from the help of God; but the choice of good or evil belongs to the man himself. (SAQ, p. 248)

These, and the countless other changes affecting every aspect of human life, have brought into being a new world of daily choices for both society and its members. What has not changed is the inescapable requirement of making such choices, whether for better or worse. It is here that the spiritual nature of the contemporary crisis comes into sharpest focus because most of the decisions called for are not merely practical but moral. (OCF, p. 5)

The sign of the intellect is contemplation and the sign of contemplation is silence, because it is impossible for a man to do two things at one time he cannot both speak and meditate.

It is an axiomatic fact that while you meditate you are speaking with your own spirit. In that state of mind you put certain questions to your spirit and the spirit answers: the light breaks forth and the reality is revealed. (PUP, page 212-13

In conclusion, the Bahá'í Writings tell us that:

- We have free will to grow and develop our spirit.

- Decisions are both practical and moral

- The views of many are better than the views of one,

- Each should contribute an opinion toward consensus.

- Consensus appears as opinions coincide.

- Our spirit reveals answers in silence

Case Story — John and Sally, Part I

I was working through a mediation with a young married couple I'll call John and Sally, and the complexity of the issues, along with the deep feelings, was slowing our progress. They seemed to have an unending list of issues and no one was willing to compromise or give an inch. I had no idea what to do next. I think our greatest insights come from our deepest frustrations.

How could you help a married couple understand one another? What would you do in this situation?

Creativity and Options

Any discussion of choice has to begin with free will. Free will is what allows us to make choices. The hardest choices to make involve the most meaningful outcomes. One of the hardest facts to accept about life is that difficulties may help our soul progress. In fact, growing through difficulty may be the only reason for physical existence, because on this physical plane we face challenges that are not available to us in the spiritual world.

The challenges that we face provide us with opportunities to develop the divine attributes that we need for the spiritual world. These divine attributes are the only things that we take with us when we leave this physical existence.

No one should go out of their way to bring calamity on themselves, but when we are presented with calamity, instead of acting out of our animal natures without thought, we can use the skills of Dynamic Consultation as a way to promote spiritual growth.

What is Subject to Free Will?

It is difficult to imagine why we have been given free will when so many people have used it to harm others. Why would a just God give men free will to do evil in the world? On the surface it seems arbitrary and cruel. But if one considers it from a deeper perspective on the meaning of life and our role in it, it becomes apparent that this physical reality is merely a stopping point — a transition — for the human spirit.

As we move through this life and develop the qualities we need, we can begin to understand that those qualities are the things that we will carry with us throughout our eternal lives. There is no way to develop this set of spiritual skills without free will. We must both desire this development and act to achieve it.

Historically, the question of free will has been whether, or to what extent, there is an external control over our actions and decisions—in other words, who is in charge? Do we make all of our own decisions, mistakes, discoveries and debacles purely through our desire and ability? Or are we puppets attached to an invisible string, all current and future events determined by some sort of karma, destiny, fate or law of nature? According to the second model we have no choice, because a higher power is in charge.

Are Destiny and Free Will Compatible?

The principle of free will has religious, ethical, and scientific implications. For example, in the religious realm, free will implies that an omnipotent divinity does not assert Its power over individual will and choices. In ethics, it implies that individuals can be held morally accountable for their actions. In the scientific realm, it implies that the actions of the body, including the brain and the mind, are not wholly determined by physical causality.

In a Bahá'í view, one reason for our free will is to develop the divine characteristics that we need for our spiritual growth. Without free will, we would never have the opportunity to develop those qualities. There would be no transformation from one state to another. If we were merely given divine qualities, we would pass through this life never having used our volition to acquire and develop them. Conversely, if those qualities were withheld from us entirely, we would have neither the knowledge of them nor the will to develop them. It is the development of those qualities that transforms us from dust mote to brilliant star — from animal to human being.

We have been given the ability to make conscious decisions that are of our own choosing. In doing so, we can help or hinder our spiritual growth. The gift of free will is the very thing that allows us to develop the divine attributes necessary both in this life and in the life to come. Free will allows us to choose to use divine guidance for our spiritual development. 9 Facets offers a program of spiritual development and goal setting by applying Baha'i principles to 9 facets of our life. See www.9facets.org/9f for more information.

What are choices?

Do we feel happy or joyful when we connect to our spiritual selves? Is happiness, itself, an indication of spiritual connection?

The best decisions do not come from a single possibility; they come from having a wide range of possibilities. Choice allows us to use our ability to reason and our free will to make better decisions. When we add values to the equation we come up with the highest and best decisions.

How can we generate choices?

Our ability to reason abstractly is one of the unique qualities of humanity. We can use our reasoning ability to make new and better choices rather than simply reacting to impulses prompted by our immediate environment. These choices can include better decision-making around reallocating resources or building stronger relationships. Ideally any good decision should do both.

Imagine

The book Imagine, by Jason Lehrer, offers some key insights into the science of our imagination. The numbers refer to pages from the book. While Lehrer was discredited for essentially plagiarizing himself, the research still remains valid.

Brain Function

Before we can have a breakthrough there has to be a block. Breakthroughs and blocks work together (7). 30 seconds before the answer erupts into consciousness there's a spike of gamma wave rhythm. We know the answer before we realize we know the answer (17).

Alpha waves direct our attention inward for insights (31). A steady rhythm of alpha waves is predictive of solving an insight puzzle up to 8 seconds before the insight arrives (30). Source of every new idea is the same - a network of neurons shifts into an unfamiliar pattern (139).

Divergent Thinking

Divergent thinking is generally associated with an inward focus and an inward focus is necessary for creative solutions. Divergent thinking trusts spontaneous epiphanies (64). Dreams enable our creativity, which is why periods of REM sleep are important when solving difficult issues (107). Subjects who dreamed during a nap resolved 40% more puzzles than those that didn't dream (107).

Social Networks

Intermediate levels of social intimacy produce the highest levels of creativity and more interactions leads to more creativity (153). Happy people are much better at guessing (32) and people who daydream more score higher on creativity (48) scales. A large number of weak social ties is more effective than a small number of strong ties (203). This is one reason why creativity levels are higher in the West than in the East.

Independence

People are less likely to explore on their own when they are given explicit instructions (236).

Convergent Thinking

Convergent thinking relies on analysis and attention (65). An outward focus is necessary for analytical solutions(31). Creativity produces many things but only judgment refines our thinking (75).

Melancholy

Melancholy sharpens the spotlight of attention (76). People in low moods remember 4 times more than those in good moods (77). Downcast moods correlate with better writing samples (77).

Animals can only react to their environment and have little influence in creating it. Humans have the unique capacities of awareness and invention. These capacities are brought into the material world through our spiritual connections. We only need to connect to the spiritual realm and divine insights will flow.

Key # 5 Expand

"...the light of reality becomes apparent when two opinions coincide." (PUP, 72-3).

Practices

Dynamic Consultation	Facilitative Mediation	World Cafe	Appreciative Inquiry	6 Hats
Expand	Options	Perspective	Dream	Green

Facilitative Mediation - Options - helping the parties create choices

Appreciative Inquiry - DREAM - People recall and identify the themes operating that contributed to the peak experience.

World Cafe - Connect Diverse Perspectives - As participants carry key ideas or themes to new tables, they exchange perspectives, greatly enriching the possibility for surprising new insights.

6 Thinking Hats Creativity (Green) - statements of provocation and investigation, seeing where a thought goes.

Skills

Man's mind, once stretched by a new idea, never regains its original dimensions.

Oliver Wendell Holmes

9 Keys	9 Skills with Questions
Expand	Brainstorm - How can we increase our choices? Reciprocity - What will do for each other?

Wisdom of Crowds offers four keys to a wise group

> 1. Diversity, represent a variety of viewpoints
> 2. Independence, not formally tied to one another
> 3. Decentralization, not physically close
> 4. Aggregation, an ability to tabulate interest
> If all 4 are present, the group can exceed the wisdom of any single individual.

Brainstorming

Traditional Brainstorming doesn't work, silent reflection is better!

Traditional group brainstorming is just not as effective as individuals are in creating new ideas. People are most creative in isolation. If creativity comes from our intellect, then we need silence to create. Group brainstorming can be used to develop and refines ideas, with honest group discussion. However, each individual should be allowed to generate the ideas in isolation and then the group should work together to improve them.

Think of brainstorming as a 2 stage process. In the first stage people engage in silent reflection over at least one period of sleep. They record their ideas over this time.

In the second stage, parties come together and debate their ideas in an open honest way. This method will offer at least 7 times more ideas and much higher quality of ideas. This is why we should have at least one period of sleep for important decisions.

See the Reciprocal Negotiation model in the case study. The parties sat in silence for 15 minutes to think of what they were willing to do and what they want the other party to do.

Traditional Brainstorming, Part 2 (see above)

If you must use a group process for brainstorming, this is the process that is typically used for generating choices on our own or during conflict resolution. There are three rules usually associated with brainstorming.

Everyone involved:

• participates from their own perspective with humility,

• accepts all positive constructive ideas, and

• doesn't judge the ideas during the discussion or draw lines of rigid demarcation.

Modern brainstorming theory says that the key to coming up with the best outcome is having the most options to choose from. If an idea is selected too quickly it probably hasn't been thoroughly developed. Effective brainstorming techniques use the following guidelines (from Participatory Decision Making, p. 100, Future search, p. 49 and 6 Thinking Hats, p. 115):

• Every contribution is worthwhile.

• Suspend judgment.

• We can modify this process before it starts or after it ends but not while its underway.

• Open minds through questioning, clarifying and summarizing.

• Ask questions to speculate, inform, show intent, feel, and test.

• Allow for the "groan zone."

A special moment in this process is called "the groan zone" (PDM) and is the point every group reaches when it feels that it has reached the end of its process without resolving the issues. Every group reaches this point and the important thing is to go on. The groan zone usually forces people out of their left brain into their right brain where they can be more creative, allowing more possible solutions to surface.

The most effective brainstorming techniques address visual, auditory and kinesthetic learning, along with right and left brain function.

Activities that work within a brainstorming process:

• Random word lists to initiate idea generation. Each person selects a random word and relates it to a specific idea in the category.

• Pass around, where everyone writes an idea on a piece of workbook and passes it to the person next to them. That person then tries to improve on the idea and it continues for 4-6 iterations. This generates many ideas very quickly.

• Add feelings, colors, animals, etc. to ideas

• Crumple up ideas on paper and throw across the room (snow ball).

• Write poem, song or skit around an idea.

• Small group discussions

• Visioning - imagine the effects of the decision in relation to another time and/or place.

• Forcefield - forces that help us and hinder us

• Gap analysis - what is between where we are now and where we need to be in the future

• Gallery walk - where everyone quietly observes what others have posted

Brainstorming generates choices that are then evaluated based on ethical criteria. But where do these new ideas come from? When we think of an idea that no one has thought of before, where did that idea originate?

Group brainstorming can be used to develop and refine ideas, with honest group discussion. However, each individual should be allowed to generate the ideas in isolation and then the group should work together to improve them.

The most effective brainstorming techniques address visual, auditory and kinesthetic learning, along with right and left brain function. There are many processes for creativity.Brainstorming generates choices that are then evaluated based on ethical criteria. But where do these new ideas come from? When we think of an idea that no one has thought of before, where did that idea originate?

Reciprocal Negotiation

Our goal in Dynamic Consultation is to generate positive productive choices. Brainstorm as many possible courses of action as possible. Be creative and consider all options.

Reciprocal negotiation is a practical process that allows each party to recognize more deeply not only their role in the situation, but the needs of the other party and their mutual obligations as well. Reciprocal negotiation is based on empathy, options and reciprocal ethics. It is a process that allows parties to explore their future in a more complete way and identify areas of agreement and areas of concern in a more focused approach. This process has aspects of brainstorming with its ability to generate options. Its framework is one in which each party is recognized and empowered.

The couple was able to use Reciprocal Negotiation to resolve their difficult relationship issues. The model used the following steps.

- After "storytelling," during which the parties expressed the situation as each saw it, I asked them to sit quietly for ten to fifteen minutes and write down at least 10 things they were willing do to resolve the situation and 10 things they would like to ask the other party to consider doing. This generated many creative ideas.

- We created a chart of Promises and Requests that each could see.

- We started in one quadrant of the chart and asked for one contribution at a time from each party as we cycled through all four quadrants (see story for example)

- We began the next round in a new quadrant and cycled through all four quadrants again. To maintain a sense of fairness, it is important to ask for only one contribution at a time in each quadrant.

• The parties were free to share any one item during their turn. If new ideas occurred during discussion, they were free to mention those during their turn.

• After at least six iterations, we started to look for matches between what one person was willing to do and what the other party was requesting.

The result was a chart in which the parties had a chance to recognize each other's needs and concerns and could address them through the actions they were willing to take and the requests they made. We ended up with very clear points of agreement and very clear points for discussion. This process is very effective for generating many viable choices.

When used in a group use the same questions with only 2 sides, with 1 side listing what individuals are willing to do and the other listing what members of the group would like to ask others to do.

Case Story — John and Sally, Part II

John and Sally needed to talk about the future of their marriage. When frustration threatened to bring us to a standstill, I stopped the interaction and asked the parties to take a few minutes and write down their thoughts. I specifically asked them each to write down what they were willing to do to help resolve the issue and then to write down what they would like to ask the other party to do. They did this in silent reflection. When they came back, they were much more focused.

This was not unexpected, because it takes 15-20 minutes for the chemicals in our body to deplete after a very emotional situation. This calming down has the added effect of allowing the other party to see the situation more clearly and come up with more creative possible solutions. The best solutions come when there are the most options available.

At this point in the process with Sally and John, I drew up a chart with the two parties on the left side and, on the right, two columns headed "what are you willing to do" and "what would you like to ask the other party to consider doing." I phrased it this way, because we can only truly commit to our own actions. We cannot control the actions of another party; we can only make humble and sincere requests. This is the Golden Rule method, when parties are offered the opportunity to consider their brother before themselves.

*Underlined options indicate cross-matches.

When we sat down together again I asked John and Sally to share one action at a time as we circled around the chart. We began in the upper left quadrant by asking John to share one thing he was willing to do in this situation. John said he was willing to take out the garbage. We then moved to ask Sally one thing she's willing to do and she was willing to go out to eat. Then moving over to the right, I asked Sally what she'd like to ask John to consider doing. Sally wanted to ask John to take out the garbage. Then moving to the upper right quadrant John wanted to ask Sally to make dinner.

	Willing to do	Ask other to consider
John	1. Take out garbage*	1. Make dinner
	2. Walk dog	2. Wash dishes
	3. Fold clothes	3. Wash laundry
Sally	1. Go out to eat	1. Take out garbage
	2. Do laundry	2. Fold clothes
	3. Wash dishes	3. Be home on time

The second trip around the chart began in the lower left quadrant, and Sally said she was willing to do laundry, but that — moving across to requests — she wanted to ask John to fold clothes. In the upper right corner John wanted to ask Sally to wash the dishes, and in the upper left quadrant John said he was willing to walk the dog.

In the third iteration, beginning with the lower right column, Sally wanted to ask John to be home on time. In the upper right corner, John wanted to ask Sally to do laundry. In the upper left corner John said he was willing to fold the clothes. And finally in the lower left quadrant, Sally was willing to wash the dishes.

As we circled the chart quadrant by quadrant for five or six cycles, we picked out cross-matches — that is, matches between what a party is willing to do and what the other party is asking of them. These were points where promises and requests lined up. For example, John wanted to ask Sally to wash the dishes and Sally said she was willing to wash the dishes. Sally was asking John to take out the garbage, which he was willing to do. He was willing to fold the clothes as she wanted to ask him to do.

However, you also notice fairly clearly the points for discussion — where a request is unmatched by a promise. Sally was interested in going out to eat but John wanted to ask her to make dinner. Only after we noted all points of agreement, did we focus more closely on the areas where there were differing options. The completed process led to very clear points of agreement and very clear points for discussion.

Whenever I do this sort of "intervention" I tell the parties that they are free to share any of the items they have written down during their turn. If new ideas occur during our discussion, they are free to mention those then. What we end up with is a flip chart where the parties have had a chance to recognize each other's needs and concerns and can address those through the actions they are willing to take and the requests they would like to make. The next step might be a written resolution to honor certain requests.

In this case, we didn't end up with a written resolution, but the couple took the flip chart home and I heard later that they posted it on the refrigerator as a reminder of their commitment. So the flip chart itself became the covenant or agreement, a reminder of their requests and promises and, ultimately, their commitment to each other.

Remember! - Create then debate.

The most important activity for generating new ideas is silent reflection. The two most important questions are: What are you willing to do? What would like to ask others to consider doing?

ELUCIDATE

Key	Goal	Move from	To
Elucidate	Virtues and Principles	Resources	Values

Elucidate is when we bring the spiritual principles to light. It also includes other decision making criteria needed to evaluate the choices. Getting to Yes says that good decisions are based on objective criteria.

Bahá'í Virtues

What is the purpose of our lives? To acquire virtues. We come from the earth; why were we transferred from the mineral to the vegetable kingdom — from the plant to the animal kingdom? So that we may attain perfection in each of these kingdoms, that we may possess the best qualities of the mineral, that we may acquire the power of growing as in the plant, that we may be adorned with the instincts of the animal and possess the faculties of sight, hearing, smell, touch and taste, until from the animal kingdom we step into the world of humanity and are gifted with reason, the power of invention, and the forces of the spirit. (PT, p. 177)

For you I desire spiritual distinction -- that is, you must become eminent and distinguished in morals. In the love of God you must become distinguished from all else. You must become distinguished for loving humanity, for unity and accord, for love and justice. In brief, you must become distinguished in all the virtues of the human world -- for faithfulness and sincerity, for justice and fidelity, for firmness and steadfastness, for philanthropic deeds and service to the human world, for love toward every hu-

man being, for unity and accord with all people, for removing prejudices and promoting international peace. Finally, you must become distinguished for heavenly illumination and for acquiring the bestowals of God. I desire this distinction for you. This must be the point of distinction among you. (PUP, p. 190)

Truthfulness, He asserts, "is the foundation of all human virtues. Without truthfulness progress and success, in all the worlds of God, are impossible for any soul. When this holy attribute is established in man, all the divine qualities will also be acquired. ('ADJ, p. 26)

Our meaning is that, in the sight of God, trustworthiness is the bedrock of His Faith and the foundation of all virtues and perfections. A man deprived of this quality is destitute of everything. ('Abdu'l-Bahá, CC, Vol. II, p. 340)

The virtues and attributes pertaining unto God are all evident and manifest, and have been mentioned and described in all the heavenly Books. (GL, p. 290)

In the same way, knowledge is a quality of man, and so is ignorance; truthfulness is a quality of man; so is falsehood; trustworthiness and treachery, justice and injustice, are qualities of man, and so forth. Briefly, all the perfections and virtues, and all the vices, are qualities of man.(SAQ, p. 236)

We ask God to endow human souls with justice so that they may be fair, and may strive to provide for the comfort of all, that each member of humanity may pass his life in the utmost comfort and welfare. Then this material world will become the very paradise of the Kingdom, this elemental earth will be in a heavenly state and all the servants of God will live in the utmost joy, happiness and gladness. We must all strive and concentrate all our thoughts in order that such happiness may accrue to the world of humanity. (FWU, p. 43)

In conclusion, the Bahá'í Writings tell us that:

The purpose of our life is unity and harmony

- through acquiring virtues such as

- faithfulness and sincerity, justice and fidelity,

- firmness and steadfastness,

- philanthropic deeds and service to the human world,

- love toward every human being,

- unity and accord with all people, removing prejudices and

- promoting international peace.

- Unity embraces all virtues.

- Unity promotes happiness.

- Truthfulness and trustworthiness are the foundation.

- We must work together to create a paradise

- where all can live in joy and happiness.

Case Story - Taking Values Off the Wall, Part I

I had the opportunity to work with a division of a major pharmaceutical company in helping them develop a more value-centered work place. They were trying to decide how to handle the distribution workload fairly. They were busier on some days than on others and they disagreed how to solve the issue. They had a corporate values statement on the wall that sounded nice, but when I asked them how to use it, no one knew. So we started to put the values into action.

What company values would you choose to resolve a difficult issue?

Virtues and Principles

The Dynamic Consultation Model is one way to demonstrate a Bahá'í approach to ethical decisions and spiritual growth. Virtues, principles and reciprocal ethics have to work together for complete solutions.

So, where do we begin?

We begin with what we believe about reality based on our understanding of our spiritual teachings. This reality revolves around the spiritual teachings of the Manifestations of God. These teaching embrace the virtues which support and inform the principles we live by and which shape reciprocal relationships. We require an edifice of virtues, principles and reciprocal ethics to completely "build" our ethical identity on this foundation. The more our decisions and actions are based on all three elements, the more meaningful they become.

Spiritually based ethical decision-making is a profoundly simple life skill that can become a compass for choice. It avoids some of the ethical difficulties with modern decision making that might focus solely on rules, maximization of benefits, selfish goals, or subjective relativism, whereby it becomes more difficult to judge a good decision.

As explained in the introduction, the Dynamic Consultation Model is about bringing together virtue ethics, principle ethics and reciprocal ethics into a single ethical paradigm.

Dynamic Consultation is a framework that yields consistent, meaningful, joyful and worthwhile decisions. Dynamic Consultation can help us acquire the spiritual attributes for our lives both for now and for the eternal spiritual realm while serving humankind today.

Values do not exist in a vacuum. There must be a standard for how we treat one another. This standard has been universally expressed by all the Manifestations of God as the Golden Rule. The Golden Rule applies to reciprocal ethics between human beings and does not refer to how we worship God. It is often expressed as treating others as you would have them treat you, or refraining from treating them in ways you would not like to be treated. Reciprocal ethics answers the question "How shall we treat one another?"

Ethics has typically been related to fields such as medicine, law or business, but an appreciation of its versatility has grown and, along with that appreciation, has come an acknowledgment that ethics encompasses all aspects of life. One needs only to think of the recent ethical difficulties with Subprime mortgages, Enron, Worldcom and Tyco to see the effects of principles without virtues. The only permanent foundations for an ethical model are the Manifestations of God, with their universal messages for humankind. This is an important point, for when principles are derived without underlying virtues, they become confusing, unstable and quickly collapse. When beliefs are derived without an underlying spiritual foundation they also collapse.

Right versus Wrong

Though clearly humanity needs virtues, principles and reciprocity, it's almost easier to understand the need for them when they aren't being practiced than to imagine what life would be like if they were.   Ethics is the process of determining right from wrong, and is the behavior that arises out of underlying beliefs and principles. As noted previously, ethics should answer the questions:

Who do I want to be (virtue ethics)?

What shall I do (principle ethics)?

How shall I treat others (reciprocal ethics)?

This may sound easy, but in reality it's a complicated task. Right and wrong are subjective concepts that vary according to culture, moral climate, and individual circumstance. What may be the right action in a particular instance may be absolutely wrong in another. Even before discussing guidelines, we need to understand the prevailing paradigms and the typical results achieved by each.

Paradigms of Moral Philosophy

There are three generally accepted paradigms of moral philosophy that are important to consider before we continue. They center either on the desired outcome, the applied rules or the degree of caring.

Paradigm 1: The first paradigm stresses the **outcome** of a behavior or action and could be summarized in the axioms "the greatest good for the greatest number," and "**the ends justify the means.**"

Paradigm 2: The second paradigm focuses on the **rules** that apply to a situation and says that you should follow the moral principles generally held by others. It could be summed up as "**the means justify the ends.**"

Paradigm 3: The third paradigm centers on **caring**, stressing the idea that **we should put others first**, as expressed in the Golden Rule.

These three paradigms of outcomes, rules and caring might typically be seen as competing with one another, but in our model we are going to look at them as partners in a process. All three are needed components in a complete, spiritually based, ethical philosophy. We need to adopt rules that result in the most beneficial outcomes for the greatest number, with a bias toward caring about what happens to all concerned. Until all three of those conditions are met, we have not acted in a completely ethical way.

Spiritual Means for Ethical Ends

The Bahá'í Faith teaches that our purpose in life is to know and worship God and follow His guidance. We do this through personal worship and reflection as well as service to humanity. This service is the vehicle for us to acquire divine attributes through knowledge of God and obedience to His laws. When we know and love God we will want to acquire the moral attributes we need for our spiritual and ethical development. Ethical decision-making allows us to develop these moral qualities through action in our outer lives which builds the divine attributes needed for our internal (and eternal) spiritual lives.

Ethical decision-making is generally defined by those who recognize the concerns of others as requiring a degree of selflessness, something difficult to grasp by those who lack the maturity to focus on anything other than their own needs and desires. Practicing ethical reflection is a mature and necessary requirement in ethical decision-making. The application of a practical ethical decision-making framework also assists the reflection process. In the case of Dynamic Consultation, the framework includes values such as respect, honesty, and caring. We would state these as behavioral goals along with the principle of the Golden Rule.

Ethical Theories

Many ethical decision-making theories have been offered historically to guide and explain individual actions.

Utilitarianism—Does this make me happy? Utilitarian theory concludes that the desire for happiness or pleasure is universal and that people intuitively view attaining their own happiness or pleasure as their ultimate goal in life.

Deontology—Am I doing my duty? Deontological theory highlights the need for individual rights to be balanced against group well-being. It stresses the importance of one's duty and following the rules.

Virtue-based —Would a good person do this? Virtue-based ethical theory focuses on the goodness or badness of people's characters.

Natural Law-based —Does this conform to the laws of nature? Natural law ethical theory supports the premise that what nature demands to be done ought to be done and when we defy nature we don't fulfill our destiny.

Rights-based —Does this support human rights? Rights-based ethical theories focus on the "rights" which must be upheld and the "wrongs" which must not be committed.

Feminist —Am I being fair to all? Feminist ethical theory centers on equality based on compassion, empathy, nurturance, and kindness.

A Bahá'í Perspective—Synthesis

From a Bahá'í perspective, the only reason for our existence is to develop the virtues and perfections we need for our eternal spiritual existence. This is an inherently virtues-based ethic. Bahá'ís would also ascribe to the deontological belief in balancing the individual and group needs, and in following the rules that have been laid down in the Kitab-i-Aqdás, the Bahá'í book of laws, with compassion and kindness. A Bahá'í ethical model requires a synthesis of utilitarian, deontological and virtue based ideologies.

Even within the theoretical categories, the study and function of ethics has been divided further. Ethicists ponder over whether we can subjectively leave what is right up to individuals or if some outside source must provide an objective and universal set of ideals.

Should these universal ideals, provided they are accepted, treat each person, event and situation the same everywhere and always? Is it more reasonable, instead, given the cultural, national and ethnic divisions in the world, to allow for a pluralistic variety of beliefs regarding right and wrong? Is right or wrong relative, for instance, and should different degrees be tolerated within limits?

The idea of limits implies that there is an objective standard against which all actions are judged. How does one sort through the morass of theory and practice to choose the best way?

You don't. It's not necessary to choose. What is missing from current theories is the possibility that they might be combined into a single model.

Bahá'í ethics would combine all aspects of these premises into a single belief that:

- There are primary moral principles

- within a diversity of individual actions

- that are bounded by acceptable limits

- based on universal virtues

- and shared by all people.

Working Together

Virtue, principle and reciprocal ethics must work together to create a complete ethical paradigm. Reciprocal Ethics without a founding virtue is not an ethic, per se, for it is merely treating someone in kind, regardless of their initial action. Thus if the initial act is kind, the reciprocal act is kind; if the initial act is unkind, so, too, is the reciprocal act. Only with virtue in play can an unkind act be reciprocated with a kind one.

Likewise, virtue by itself without reciprocal ethics fails to rise to the level of an ethic. It is like a beautiful work of art that no one has ever seen or a tool that remains hidden in the toolbox and is never used. However, when an action is reciprocated based on a virtue, this is the highest form of interaction and all parties have the opportunity to grow and learn. Thus, virtue becomes the guide for reciprocal action; reciprocation becomes the means for the demonstration of virtue.

In summary:

Values include both virtues (beliefs) and principles (standards).

Virtue Ethics deals with attributes, character, qualities or beliefs—**who we are.**

Principle Ethics deals with standards, ethical guidelines or action—**what we do.**

Reciprocal Ethics is the Golden Rule of social exchange—**how we interact.**

Complete Ethical Paradigm

All three of these are needed for a sustainable ethical paradigm. Virtue without action is like a beautiful empty vase; nice, but not useful.

Principles without virtue are short term fixes which will not sustain themselves over time. They seem logical, but lack foundation.

Reciprocity without virtues or principles will not result in healthy relationships. Treating another the same as you want to be treated doesn't take into account that your character or your principles might not be praiseworthy.

Many great thinkers have given us their ideas about virtues and courage is a recurring theme. Here is a sampling:

One isn't necessarily born with courage, but one is born with potential. Without courage you cannot practice any other virtue with consistency. We can't be kind, true, merciful, generous or honest.

- Maya Angelou

With courage you will dare to take risks, have the strength to be compassionate, and the wisdom to be humble. Courage is the foundation of integrity.

- Keshavan Nair

Gratitude is not only the greatest of virtues, but the parent of all the others.

- Cicero

Compassion is the basis of morality.

- Arnold Schopenhauer

Peace is not the absence of war; it is a virtue; a state of mind; a disposition for benevolent confidence; and justice.

- Spinoza

We need to find the right balance for any virtue. For example, moderation is what guides us to be courageous instead of rash or cowardly, grateful instead of ungrateful or insincere, compassionate instead of uncaring or overly protective, peaceful instead of violent or tolerant.

Too Little	Virtue	Too Much
Cowardice	Courage	Rashness
Ungrateful	Gratitude	Insincere
Uncaring	Compassionate	Overly protective
Violence	Peace	Tolerance

Moral Development

Man's physical existence on this earth is a period during which the spiritual exercise of his free will is tried and tested in order to prepare his soul for the other worlds of God, and we must welcome affliction and tribulations as opportunities for improvement in our eternal selves.('Abdu'l-Bahá, LOG, p. 367)

In the secular world, moral development takes place in an individual through informal and formal education. The work of the educational psychologist Lawrence Kohlberg and others shows that there may be a universal process of moral development. Kohlberg contends that "the same basic ways of moral valuing are found in every culture and develop in the same order." He states that there is a developmental process involving five, possibly six, stages. To him, justice lies at the heart of moral development, and the principles of justice are the forms by which moral conflicts are resolved.

Kohlberg studied the process of moral reasoning and showed how, over the years, children and young adults move through the following stages of moral development, one after another, believing that what is "right" is:

1) What they can get away with without being punished;

2) Anything that serves their immediate self-interest;

3) That which gains them social approval;

4) What the laws and rules say is right;

5) What is reciprocally agreed upon as fair;

6) That which is consistent with universal principles of justice and ethics.

The researchers demonstrated that when young people were exposed to moral reasoning levels one stage higher than their own, they typically moved to the next stage; while thankfully, the person at the higher moral reasoning level did not regress to a lower stage. It seems our moral progress is preset to advance.

Note the connection of Stage 6, the highest stage, with universal human values and universal ethics. Kohlberg further speculated that a seventh stage might exist which would link religion with moral reasoning. However, because of Kohlberg's trouble providing empirical evidence for even a sixth stage, he emphasized that his conjecture about a seventh stage was purely theoretical. As Bahá'ís, we know that there is definitely a seventh stage and we aim directly at it.

Virtue Ethics

Virtue ethics are more than a matter of rules; it is also a matter of ideals. Rules indicate which activities are forbidden, permitted or required, whereas ideals encourage us to take the high road even when there are no rules governing the situation, or when we do not know what rules are in operation.

This brings up another saying: In a just society laws are unneeded; in an unjust society they are unenforceable. For humankind to mature we must move beyond laws which punish wrong actions to moral guidance which encourages the best of actions.

Where virtue is at stake, compliance is not enough. Only continual striving to be a good human is acceptable. At this level, moral virtues become true action rather than reaction to external forces such as hope for reward or fear of punishment.

A Combined List

If we consider virtues from different sources we end up with this combined list. Institute for Global Ethics (I), livingvalues.net (L), the Boy Scout by-laws (B),The Virtues Guide (V), and Managing with the Wisdom of Love (M) each contain virtues. If we combine them we see that nineteen sets of virtues are mentioned in at least two out of four of those sources.

Cleanliness – B, V

Consideration and Cooperation – L, V

Bravery and Courage – B, V

Courtesy – B, V

Friendliness, Gratitude and Love – B, L, V

Helpfulness – B, V

Honesty and Truthfulness – I, L, V

Humility and Forbearance – L, V, M

Joyfulness Cheerfulness Happiness– B, L, V

Kindness, Mercy and Compassion – I, B, V

Moderation, Thrift and Simplicity – B, L, V

Obedience, Loyalty, Firmness, Fidelity – B, V

Peacefulness – L, V

Respect – I, L, V, M

Responsibility – I, L, V

Reverence and Faithfulness – B, V

Self- Discipline and Freedom – L, V

Trustworthiness and Sincerity – B, V, M

Unity – L, V, M

These commonly accepted virtues can be the starting point for ethical decision making, and we will use them as criteria as we develop Dynamic Consultation.

Is it a virtue or a principle?

There isn't necessarily a clean line between virtues and principles. There are virtues that can also be principles, such as cleanliness and reverence. Cleanliness can refer to a physical surrounding or to a state of mind. Reverence can be an inner quality or an outward action. However, for the sake of this book, when we refer to virtues, we mean those inner qualities that influence our character, and when we say principles we mean outward actions.

Not all virtues carry equal weight in a given situation, nor do all situations need to use every virtue for resolution. Once we understand the need for virtues, the next question is which virtue takes priority. For example, Baha'is say that truthfulness is at the top, Cicero says gratitude comes first, Nair prefers courage. In choosing virtues, one must place them in whatever order the situation warrants. It's not that we disagree about what virtues are important; rather our challenge is to decide which ones to apply to a given situation and how to prioritize them.

Principle Ethics

Principle ethics answers the question, "What shall I do?" Principle ethics are the practical guidance often found within a profession that is referred to as professional guidelines or professional codes of conduct. They allow us to take consistent, meaningful action around a difficult decision. Underlying all principle ethics are virtues. Principles without virtues will not stand long by themselves. Aristotle, a virtue ethicist, embraced practical wisdom as a way for reason to lead to action.

Spiritual principles are more than practical solutions and good intentions. They guide our spirit and are in line with the very purpose of our life. We can find solutions for every social problem by applying spiritual principles.

Consider that the worst of qualities and most odious of at-tributes, which is the foundation of all evil, is lying. No worse or more blameworthy quality than this can be imagined to exist; it is the destroyer of all human perfections, and the cause of innumer-able vices. There is no worse characteristic than this; it is the foundation of all evils. Notwithstanding all this, if a doctor con-soles a sick man by saying: "Thank God you are better, and there is hope of your recovery," though these words are contrary to the truth, yet they may become the consolation of the patient and the turning-point of the illness. This is not blameworthy. (SAQ, p. 215-16)

There are also selective violations of the principles that society considers acceptable. Killing is illegal, unless we are fighting a "just war." Lying is wrong, unless we are telling a child about the Tooth Fairy, or saving them from harm, and so on. These interpre-tive variations cause people to conclude that there are no univer-sal standards for ethics, and that moral responsibility is relative to cultural practices. This is a dangerous conclusion that relieves us of any responsibility other than what we choose in our own inter-ests, what has been dictated by the rules of our faiths or govern-ments, our personal values, or the local status quo.

As we have seen, there are universal and seemingly self-evi-dent virtues and principles common to a wide variety of cultures. These can be practiced in many different ways. For example, vir-tually all cultures value trustworthiness; but they have different views on truth-telling. This is illustrated by Eastern versus West-ern preferred values for harmony (keeping the peace) versus forthrightness (telling the truth even if it hurts). Someone from an Eastern culture might demonstrate politeness by withholding their real thoughts on a matter, while a person from a Western cul-ture may feel this is unnecessarily cautious and, putting truthful-ness ahead of harmony, would be more forthright. Both cultures agree in principle that deceit is unethical and trustworthiness is ethical, but misunderstandings can arise when the underlying principle is embodied in ways that reflect diverse cultural values and virtues.

To cite another, even more basic example, take courtesy — which Bahá'u'lláh lauds as the "prince of virtues." All cultures prize courtesy, but have different understandings of what it is. The Middle-Eastern custom of standing very close to someone in conversation — which is an expression of courteous openness — can seem intimidating and off-putting to a Westerner. Both cultures agree in principle that courtesy is an important virtue, but do not agree about what courtesy looks like in practice.

These principles are simply recurring patterns of ethically responsible behavior with a different outward appearance. As elements in solving a problem cross-culturally, they may require some investigation and explanation so that the parties can arrive at a mutually agreed framework for understanding the practice of a particular virtue.

What are principle ethics?

The Bahá'í International Community has proposed five spiritual principles that lie at the foundation of a global civilization. These are summarized in their statement <u>Valuing Spirituality in Development</u> (VSD).

Based on the vision of a just, united and sustainable global civilization, five spiritual principles that are foundational to the realization of such a future are presented. While they are by no means the only principles necessary to consider, it is felt that these five contain a sufficient diversity of concepts to serve as the starting point for this effort. The five principles are:

- *unity in diversity*

- *equity and justice*

- *equality of the sexes*

- *trustworthiness and moral leadership*

- *independent investigation of truth*

Two spiritual principles that might be part of an extended list are beauty and service.

How can Principle Ethics be used?

When principal ethics are based on virtues, they have a much higher quality.

· They are sustainable in that they are generated instinctively and internally and not reliant on external conditions.

· They are transcendent, meaning that they aren't only for today, they will last well into the future.

· Any actions taken based on them will also be more clearly justifiable and rest on a solid logical footing.

· They are transferable, in that they can be applied to many different situations. They should work just as well in sales and marketing as they do in human resources.

· They are a positive motivating force and inspire people to go beyond the minimum requirements.

· They are unifying. They form a common set of goals, shared by a group of people. They are a way to think and act together. The principles themselves can become a source of unifying goals for a community.

Principle ethics which are not based on virtues present a number of challenges. They may be empirically based in societal consensus and are thus guided by a relativistic model that has no firm anchor. They may be based on anecdotal stories that seem right, but do not have a broader application than to the specific situation. They may form only a set of behavioral guidelines with material objectives that do not go beyond regulating misbehavior.

Principles that don't arise out of virtues often promote social order over social justice and look to maintain the status quo in any setting. They are merely short-term solutions for long-term problems and will not stand the test of time. They may appear as a menu, with a hierarchical listing of inappropriate behavior. A person might look at such a list (there are many sins but only seven deadly sins) and comfort themselves that while they cheated, at least they didn't lie. These principles may look a lot like laws in that they might be designed only to discourage maleficent action rather than encourage beneficent action.

Unfortunately, principle ethics that are not based on virtues may look only as deep as people are comfortable going because to peer more deeply into one's pool of virtues (perhaps finding it half-empty) requires what can be an uncomfortable level of self-knowledge and self-assessment.

Personal Principle Ethics

Personal principle ethics might also be called morality, since they reflect general expectations of any person in any society, acting in any capacity. One definition of culture says "culture is what everyone knows that everyone else knows." These are the principles we try to instill in our children, and expect of one another without needing to articulate the expectation or formalize it in any way.

Principles of Personal Ethics include:

· Concern for the well-being of others, doing good (beneficence)

· Respect for the personal space and independence of others (autonomy)

· Trustworthiness & honesty (fidelity)

· Willing compliance with the law, except for civil disobedience (justice)

· Basic justice; being fair (justice)

· Preventing harm (non-maleficence)

Exercise the Virtues We Expect of Others

Principles can only provide guidance. When exploring an ethical dilemma, you will still have to examine the situation to see how each of the above principles may relate to that particular situation. At times this alone will clarify the issues enough that the means for resolving the dilemma will become obvious to you. Yet, there are myriad situations that will never lend themselves to an easy formula, and sometimes the principles can only be used to trigger our conscience, not guide our decisions.

There will be times when principles collide with other principles. In more complicated cases it is helpful to be able to work through the steps of an ethical decision-making model, and to assess which of these moral principles may be in conflict. If two or more principles are in conflict you need to decide which is the guiding principle that trumps or informs all others.

It is important to note that principles of personal ethics are the first checkpoint we cross in any situation. They often override those at the professional and global levels. For example, we need to be trustworthy on a personal level before we can expect someone to trust us or to behave in a trustworthy manner toward us. We need to exercise the virtues and principles we expect of others.

In attempting to globalize issues for the parties involved in a dispute or a moral dilemma and look at the situation from the broadest possible perspective, the parties might want to consider the ethics that guide other cultures and communities, as well as their own. They might also want to consider promoting better actions among people, in not doing what is expected, but in doing what is better than expected.

Professional Principle Ethics

Most professions are guided by model standards or ethical guidelines. These principles are designed to help professionals resolve practice-related issues and can be used to clarify and define appropriate responses to most situations.

Kitchener (1984), a counseling psychologist, has identified five moral principles that are viewed as the cornerstone of most ethical guidelines. Though ethical guidelines cannot address all situations that we are forced to confront, reviewing these ethical principles can help clarify the issues involved in a given situation. The five principles — autonomy, justice, beneficence, non-maleficence, and fidelity — are considered self-evident truths in that they are obvious in and of themselves.

Autonomy is the principle that addresses the idea of independence. The essence of this principle is allowing an individual the freedom of choice and action.

Non-maleficence is the idea of not causing harm to others. Often explained as "above all do no harm," it also reflects both the idea of not inflicting intentional harm, and not engaging in actions that risk harming others accidentally.

Beneficence reflects our responsibility to contribute to the welfare of each other. Simply stated it means to do good proactively.

Justice does not mean treating all individuals the same, it means treating equals equally and unequals unequally but in proportion to their relevant differences.

Fidelity involves the notions of loyalty, faithfulness, and honoring commitments. We must be able to trust each other and have faith in our relationships if growth is to occur.

By exploring a given dilemma in regard to these principles one may come to a better understanding of the conflicting issues.

The following is a comparison of ethical guidelines within several specific professions. These written codes provide rules of conduct and standards of behavior based on the principles of professional ethics. Even when not written into a code, principles of professional ethics are usually expected of people in a professional capacity. See the chart that follows.

Reviewing these ethical principles helps to clarify the issues involved in a given situation. The five principles are each self-evident. By examining any dilemma through the lens of these principles one may come to a better understanding of the conflicting issues, arrive at better decisions or be more capable of analyzing past actions. As with personal ethics, when exploring an ethical dilemma in this arena, you need to examine the situation and see how each principle relates to it.

Individuals acting in a professional capacity take on an additional burden of ethical responsibility. For example, professional associations have codes of ethics that prescribe required behavior within the context of a professional practice such as medicine, law, accounting, or engineering. Even when not written into a code, principles of professional ethics are usually expected of business people, employees, volunteers, elected representatives and so on.

This chart illustrates the similarity between different sets of professional principles. Kitchener (1984), identified the 5 principles in the publication *Counseling Psychologist*.

Kitchener	Medicine	Mediation	School Counselors	Bahá'í
Beneficence	Beneficence	Competence	Encourage maximum development	Equality
Non-maleficence	Non-maleficence	No harm to self/others	No harm to self/others	Unity in diversity
Autonomy	Autonomy	Self-Determination	Right to choose	Independent investigation of truth
Justice	Fairness	Impartiality	Fairness	Equity and justice
Fidelity	Confidential	Confidential	Confidential	Trustworthiness and Moral Leadership

Reciprocity

Bahá'í Quotes

On the contrary, man cannot live singly and alone. He is in need of continuous cooperation and mutual help. For example, a man living alone in the wilderness will eventually starve. He can never, singly and alone, provide himself with all the necessities of existence. Therefore, he is in need of cooperation and reciprocity.
(FWU, p. 38)

Of like kind are the relationships that exist among all created things. Hence it was stated that cooperation and reciprocal ethics are essential properties which are inherent in the unified system of the world of existence, and without which the entire creation would be reduced to nothingness. (Huq, p. 22)

...we should cast aside all the prejudices of ignorance, discard superannuated beliefs in traditions of past ages and raise aloft the banner of international agreement. Let us cooperate in love and, through spiritual reciprocal ethics, enjoy eternal happiness and peace. (PUP, p. 380)

It is evident, therefore, that the foundation of real brother-hood, the cause of loving cooperation and reciprocity, and the source of real kindness and unselfish devotion is none other than the breaths of the Holy Spirit....When human brotherhood is founded upon the Holy Spirit, it is eternal, changeless, unlimited.
(PUP, p. 392)

In conclusion, the Bahá'í Writings tell us that:
- We cannot live alone
- We need cooperation and reciprocity
- Without cooperation, the world would be reduced to nothingness.
- Spiritual reciprocal ethics will lead to eternal happiness and peace. When human brotherhood is founded upon the Holy Spirit, it is eternal, changeless, unlimited.

Reciprocal Ethics

Reciprocal ethics is about the equation of giving and receiving. Truly ethical behavior, according to the Bahá'í Writings, should give more than it receives. The foundation of reciprocal ethics is a general philosophical principle common to all religious and moral codes, often as a fundamental rule. The most common formulation, known as The Golden Rule, is found in every religion and thus exists in most cultures, at least in the abstract.

Why are reciprocal ethics important?

Reciprocity is a vital ingredient in the world of existence, for without it "the entire creation would be reduced to nothingness". Reciprocal ethics will cause eternal happiness and peace, and real brotherhood, kindness and unselfish devotion. Its foundation is the breath of the Holy Spirit.

What are reciprocal ethics?

We ought always to deal justly, not only with those who are just to us, but likewise to those who endeavor to injure us; and this, for fear lest by rendering them evil for evil, we should fall into the same vice.   — Hierocles

Reciprocal ethics should not be confused with tit for tat, revenge, an eye for an eye, retributive justice or the law of retaliation. The ethic of reciprocal ethics is not about retaliation; it is about treating others with the same — or greater — respect and consideration as one wishes to be treated. A key element of the ethic of reciprocal ethics is that a person attempting to live by this rule treats all people, not just members of his or her "in" group, with consideration.

In considering reciprocal ethics and how we relate to the world around us, we begin with the mind. As we saw in Key 3, Explore, if we look at the mind as the intermediary between the spiritual and the physical world around us we can think of the brain as our spiritual connection. Instead of being a single function-switching mechanism the brain becomes an adaptable, intelligent port for the transmission of experiences from the physical to the spiritual, and concepts from the spiritual to the material. This exchange is vital, for without it we would never grow and develop.

We know that we have the capacity to, spontaneously and of our own accord, bring about willful action where we create a sense of self through the interaction between the material world and our inner spiritual reality. When we talk about the purpose of our lives as that of acquiring the divine virtues, we are asked to use all the spiritual and physical resources available to us to develop a praiseworthy character. We are given the innate desire to grow and develop both as individuals, and collectively as a society. If this desire were missing, we would not have grown as a society. So the growth of society proves the existence of the desire.

Reciprocal ethics is one manifestation of our desire to grow. Reciprocal ethics begins with how we perceive and process the world around us. We'll begin by looking at the Golden Rule, and how it guides our actions.

The Golden Rule

The teaching that we should treat others as we ourselves would wish to be treated, an ethic variously repeated in all the great religions, sums up the moral attitude, the peace-inducing aspect, extending through these religions irrespective of their place or time of origin; it also signifies an aspect of unity which is their essential virtue, a virtue mankind in its disjointed view of history has failed to appreciate. (PWP, p. 4)

The Golden Rule, the teaching that we should treat others as we ourselves would wish to be treated, is an ethic at the heart of religion. As man has evolved so has the Golden Rule. What first started as a justification for punishment has transformed into altruistic service.

The Golden Rule has four distinct evolutions:

1. An eye for an eye - the original Biblical admonition as a way to right wrongs. This is an equal exchange of harm.

2. Don't harm others in ways that would they would find harmful - Krishna, Confucius, Buddha, Zoroaster and Moses. This says do not harm others.

3. Do for others what you would want done for you - Krishna, Jesus and Mohammed. This says to do for others what you would want done for you.

1. "Blessed is he who preferreth his brother before himself."
   Bahá'u'lláh — TAB, p. 71. This says to do more for others than you would do for yourself.

The interfaith declaration entitled "Towards a Global Ethic," which was produced by an assembly of religious and spiritual leaders from virtually every major world religion and spiritual movement at the 1993 Parliament of the World's Religions in Chicago, suggests that it is indeed possible for the world's religions to find much common ground in this regard.

The declaration states: "We affirm that a common set of core values is found in the teachings of the religions, and that these form the basis of a global ethic... There already exist ancient guidelines for human behavior which are found in the teachings of the religions of the world and which are the condition for a sustainable world order."

Golden Rule is a principle ethic based on the reciprocal actions of the parties with no requirement of an underlying belief system. By itself, it serves a purpose for interpersonal relationships. When you use spiritual virtues and principles, along with the Golden Rule, you have a guide for Dynamic Consultation and for spiritual development.

The Golden Rules

Buddhism: "Hurt not others in ways that you yourself would find hurtful." — Udana-Varqa, 5:18

Zoroastrianism: "That nature only is good when it shall not do unto another whatever is not good for its own self." — Dadistan-i Dinik, 94:5

Judaism: "What is hateful to you, do not to your fellow men. That is the entire Law, all the rest is commentary." — The Talmud, Shabbat, 31a

Hinduism: "This is the sum of all true righteousness: deal with others as thou wouldst thyself be dealt by. Do nothing to thy neighbor which thou wouldst not have him do to thee after." — The Mahabharata

Christianity: "As ye would that men should do to you, do ye also to them likewise." — Luke 6:31

Islam: "No one of you is a believer until he desires for his brother that which he desires for himself." — Sunnah

Confucianism: "Surely it is the maxim of loving-kindness: Do not unto others that you would not have them do unto you." — Analects, XV, 23

Bahá'í Faith: "He should not wish for others that which he doth not wish for himself, nor promise that which he doth not fulfill." — GL, p. 266

"Blessed is he who preferreth his brother before himself." TAB, 71

This Golden Rule is meant to inform exchanges between two or more parties and is intended for the giver. It requires at least an equal exchange for the parties. Competition is a form of exchange when one party takes more than they give. Cooperation is when both parties give the same. Collaboration is when one or both parties unselfishly gives more than is required for the good of all concerned.

The Golden Rule refers to a cooperative exchange, except for the last Bahá'í rule, which states that you should prefer the other to yourself, which is a collaborative exchange.

An eye for an eye was an improvement for society at the time it was enunciated, because before that it was a life for an eye. The Golden Rule improved society further because it discouraged unequal distribution.

Scripture now asks us to consider blessed those that recognize their own needs and the needs of others, and place the other's needs ahead of their own. How can reciprocal ethics be used?

From Theory to Practice

The previous sections have shared a number of ethical theories as a way of demonstrating the inclusive value of a Bahá'í model of ethical decision making. Theories show categories of collective thought which can be infinitely divided and focused according to the needs and desires of the cultural group.

However, to go from theory to practice, one must stop theorizing and start using the collective wisdom of the past and present to move forward into a more functional future. Though primarily exploring these practices in groups, similar techniques can be used by individuals.

A more thorough exploration of the individual process of decision-making and goal setting can be found in Spirit Journey— Creating a Praiseworthy Life, available from 9-Facets Publishing at www.9facets.org/9f.

Key #6 Elucidate

Man must strive that his reality may manifest virtues and perfections (WT, p. 13)

Practices

Dynamic Consultation	Facilitative Mediation	World Cafe	Appreciative Inquiry	6 Hats
Elucidate	Criteria			

Facilitative Mediation - Criteria - Selecting the criteria for agreeing on how to judge a good decision.

Skills

Whenever two good people argue over principles, they are both right. - Marie Ebner Von Eschenbach

9 Keys	9 Skills with Questions
Elucidate	Wisdom - What does society say?
	Value Scan - What values are important to us?

Wisdom

Wisdom is considering what wise people have said about this issue. Look to people you respect like your grand parents, your co-workers or your neighbors. How would they vie this situation? What advice would they offer?

Value Scan

Criteria is not commonly used in most processes for judging the quality of a decision. Most modern decision making is relativistic and based on selecting the best course available. Criteria judges the courses available and that creates additional challenges, but also offers more comprehensive and sustainable decisions.

Criteria are one of the most valuable ways to make a decision. We use criteria all of the time, even though more practices don't recognize it. Criteria can be cost or time, or ir could be our values.

In order to use values in the decision making process we need to identify the values that are important to each member of the group. We might do this with what I call a Value Scan. Consider the answers to these questions. Identify the virtues and principles you feel are important to consider in this situation.

What virtues am I developing with this action? What do I see as the most important virtues for my personal growth? (virtues)

What principles can be used to evaluate this issue? What principles would be used by someone I admire? (principles)

How is this issue affecting others? How would they like to be treated? (reciprocity)

Use the answers to these questions in the next section on evaluation.

Rational Criteria

Along with virtues and principles, we need to also consider the rational criteria. These criteria might include cost, time, commitment and resources. The more objective the criteria, the easier it is to justify the decision. The Evaluation section will show how to use criteria in evaluating options.

Case Story — Taking Values Off the Wall, Part II

We decided to use the company value statement to guide our decision making process. It was conveniently posted on the wall in our meeting room. First we broke the statement into virtues and principles. These values included:

Virtues (who you are) = Integrity*, respect, honesty

Principles (what you do) = Quality, innovation*, teamwork, customer focus*, leadership, performance.

Since we were going to use the company values to resolve this problem, we considered which values should be used. The main issue was using overtime to fill orders in the warehouse. We came up with six different possible solutions. We then used the corporate value statement to evaluate the options. We decided to use the values of integrity, innovation and customer focus as our guiding values. We looked at ranking the options by how much it supported the value and asked if the option was a positive reflection of the value. We were not done until we had an option that at least positively addressed each appropriate value. These were the five choices that we generated using the skills from the Expand chapter.

Option 1 – work overtime

Option 2 – let orders carryover to next day

Option 3 – hire temporary help to work

Option 4 – prioritize orders based on sales

Option 5 – Integrate live ordering with shipping time

We looked at each option in relation to the values in the columns. The option either supported the value (+), was neutral to the value (0), or diminished the value (-). None of the first four options (1-4) supported both integrity and customer focus. When we continued to search for options we found an option (5) that supported all of the values.

Option	Integrity	Innovation	Customer focus
1	+	O	+
2	-	O	-
3	-	-	+
4	+	O	+
5	+	+	+

They put their values into action and ended up with a much better decision. This exercise resulted in a more meaningful values statement and one that could then be modified based on experience instead of hung on a wall and forgotten. The point here is that you shouldn't stop looking for options until you have found at least one that addresses all of your values.

Remember!

Select the criteria that mean the most to you and others.

In the next section we will see how to use those values to help guide the decision making process.

EVALUATE

Key	Goal	Move from	To
Evaluate	Options and Criteria	Voting	Spectrums

In evaluation, we compare the choices with the values and other positive criteria, including resources, and relationships. Look for opportunities where the principles and the options are in closest alignment.

Bahá'í Quotes -

There are spiritual principles, or what some call human values, by which solutions can be found for every social problem. Any well-intentioned group can in a general sense devise practical solutions to its problems, but good intentions and practical knowledge are usually not enough. The essential merit of spiritual principle is that it not only presents a perspective which harmonizes with that which is immanent in human nature, it also induces an attitude, a dynamic, a will, an aspiration, which facilitate the discovery and implementation of practical measures. Leaders of governments and all in authority would be well served in their efforts to solve problems if they would first seek to identify the principles involved and then be guided by them.
(PWP, p. 2)

In conclusion, the Bahá'í Writings tell us that:

• We use spiritual principles for solving social problems.

• A good principle presents a perspective and a dynamic which facilitates practical measures.

Case Story — Strategic Principles out of Court, Part I

Choice plays a critical role in large complex issues. I was working with our Regional Planning Governing Board in a situation in which they had to develop strategic planning principles for the master plan for our community. This group was made up of three governmental entities which had sued one another off and on over a period of years. They needed new and more creative ways to look at the planning principles they wanted to adopt.

They had 120 principles to agree on and the work in a public meeting would be overwhelming. However, giving them a simple choice was the answer.

How were we going to take on such an overwhelming problem? Was there a simpler way to break it down?

Options and Criteria

Once we have identified the issues involved and created choices, we should decide on the ethical principles and virtues that are appropriate to the situation. We should then use these values when we are ready to evaluate our options. Our values are our highest level of belief; they represent our ethical unity, the areas where we all should be able to agree.

Ethics are values in action. Ethical decision making models use the values of the parties as a way to evaluate options.

Principled Decision Making

Your task is not to seek love, but merely to seek and find all the barriers within yourself that you have built against it.

— Rumi

Ethical decisions allow for the integration of virtue, principle and reciprocity. Ethics is the outcome of using virtues and principles to evaluate available choices. It is a way to appraise our options and make decisions based on our values. Principled decision-making allows involved parties the unique opportunity of working together to decide on a better future.

How do we teach the skill of making positive choices?

One element is the introduction of criteria to the decision-making process. Decision-making criteria are the factors that differentiate one choice from another. They can include tangibles such as time, human resources or money, Virtues or Principles, or any combination thereof. The criteria you choose will determine the quality of your decision.

To arrive at a criterion for principled decision-making, you might ask a series of questions.

Is your decision:

- representative of your values — your virtues and principles?

- likely to make you a better person?

- one you'd be comfortable with if your family or co-workers were observing you?

- one you'd be comfortable with if your actions were widely publicized (thereby serving as the only way that some people know you)?

- likely to improve the relationship of the parties involved?

- likely to withstand scrutiny?

- one that shows leadership through integrity, accountability and efficiency?

- fair to yourself, family, colleagues, industry and/or community?

These are just a few questions you could ask yourself when considering the choices of a difficult decision. The point is to ask the right question at the right time. History is filled with examples of people who asked the wrong question at the wrong time, or didn't ask a question at all.

- Decide which principles apply to the specific situation, and determine which principle takes priority for you or your group. Consult any experts or professional associations to see if they can provide help with the dilemma.

- After you have clarified the problem, refer to your own professional Code of Ethics to see if the issue is addressed there. If there is an applicable standard (or several) that are specific and clear, following the course of action indicated should lead to a resolution of the problem. To be able to apply such ethical standards, it is essential to read them carefully and to understand their implications.

- If the problem is more complex and a resolution does not seem apparent, then you probably have a true ethical dilemma and need to continue with further steps in the ethical decision-making process.

Point of Consensus

Consensus is defined as a collective agreement. Consensus ranges from strong to weak. As long as everyone is at the same point you can have consensus at either end of the spectrum. The keys to achieving strong consensus is:

· having complete information,

· having a clear understanding of the issues,

· giving full consideration of all parties' perspectives,

· fully exploring all options

· having a range of potential resolutions.

Vote

Consensus processes use voting as a last resort. If the issue is complex, break it down into component parts. If consensus is unattainable, the process might call for a vote to be taken.

A vote, however, gives little information about the level of commitment of the group. Are the people voting 51% in favor of it or 99%? Instead of asking who is in favor of the proposal why not ask who has time and would like to work on implementing it. What is the point of approving excellent ideas if no one is willing to put them into action? Think of spectrums rather than yes or no.

Remember that there are two types of voting: preference and selection. In preference, items are given a priority to be able to facilitate discussion. In selection, items are chosen for implementation.

Principles versus Absolute Rules and Universality

It is tempting to apply Principles selectively, or only within set boundaries, but limiting the application of ethical Principles negates their value. Ethical Principles must apply to everyone, everywhere, anytime. However, when considering a hierarchy of values, occasionally one may take priority over another. For example, there are situations in which compassion may come before truth. A doctor may relieve unnecessary suffering and even offer hope by consoling the ill with half-truths.

From Principle to Action

Once we have identified the issues involved we need decide on the spiritual principles and virtues that are appropriate to the situation. These values should then be used in the evaluation step of options. Our values are our highest level of belief and represent our spiritual unity, which are areas we all should be able to agree on.

The choices we make determine our ethical growth. Once we have generated potential choices we need to identify the decision-making criteria, virtues, principles and reciprocity, and consider the potential consequences of all options in relation to those criteria. From this process, we can determine a course of action.

Before you act ask yourself:

· Consider the information you have gathered and the priorities you have set.

· Evaluate each option and assess the potential consequences for all the parties.

· Ponder the implications of each course of action for those who will be affected, and for your organization or community.

· Eliminate the options that clearly do not give the desired results or cause consequences that are even more problematic.

· Review the remaining options to determine which option or combination of options best fits the situation, and addresses the priorities you have identified.

· Review the selected course of action to see if it presents any new ethical considerations.

If the course of action you have selected seems to present new ethical issues, perhaps you have chosen the wrong option or you might have identified the problem incorrectly.

Key # 7 - Evaluation

There are spiritual principles, or what some call human values, by which solutions can be found for every social problem.

PUP, p.28

Practices

Dynamic Consultation	Facilitative Mediation	World Cafe	Appreciative Inquiry	6 Hats
Evaluate	Selection	Pattern	Design	Yellow Black

Facilitative Conflict Resolution - Selection - deciding which options best meet the criteria

Appreciative Inquiry - DESIGN - People write how the organization functions in the present.

World Cafe - Listen together for Patterns and Insights - Encourage people to listen for what is not being spoken along with what is being shared.

6 Thinking Hats Discernment (Black) - logic applied to identifying reasons to be cautious and conservative

6 Thinking Hats Optimistic response (Yellow) - logic applied to identifying benefits, seeking harmony

Participatory Decision Making builds consensus by creating and clarifying ideas through spectrums.

Skills

There are many more wrong answers than right ones, and they are easier to find.

Michael Friedlander

9 Keys	9 Skills with Questions
Evaluate	Matrix - How can we use our criteria and options? Spectrums - How do we feel about our options?

6 Methods for Evaluation

Here are 6 methods for criteria based decision making. The only binding method is the vote. All the other methods can offer any number of choices and are part of working toward consensus. The criteria for all of these could include, virtues, principles and reciprocity (ethical decision making), resources, time, frequency or any objective criteria.

Will work/won't work - asks the parties to identify all the reasons an idea will or won't work. When the supporters realize why an idea won't work and the detractors realize why an idea will work, you can have real breakthroughs.

Spectrum - stand or group together to show preference from weak to strong support

Rating - according to an objective measuring system

Ranking - indicate a preference order, however this doesn't show support

Preference - indicates support, + indicates a preference, 0 is non-committal, - is is not preferred

Vote - when all else fails, use 2 choices, yes/no. Votes give little information and no choice, but does give a decision. Consensus processes use voting as a last resort. Before voting, be sure the question is stated completely. If the issue is complex, break it down into component parts. If consensus is unattainable, the process might call for a vote to be taken.

A vote, however, gives little information about the level of commitment of the group. Are the people voting 51% in favor of it or 99%? Instead of asking who is in favor of the proposal why not ask who has time and would like to work on implementing it. What is the point of approving excellent ideas if no one is willing to put them into action? Think in terms of spectrums rather than yes or no.

Remember that there are two types of voting: preference and selection. In preference, items are given a priority in order to be able to facilitate discussion. In selection, items are chosen for implementation.

Spectrums

Spectrums can be used in many different ways. Spectrums are ask people to stand in a line based on a spectrum of choices. If you need to decide how much money to spend, ask people to stand in line based on their preference. If you have any numerical decision, use a spectrum. If you want to see how much support there is for an idea, use a spectrum. Once people are standing ask them why they are standing there. See if the option can be modified. What happens to levels of support as it changes?

A spectrum gives much information very quickly. When you have reached the point for a decision, ask people to stand in line from warm to hot support. When everyone stands at hot support, you have consensus and the decision will be implemented. If everyone is lukewarm, see if you can modify the proposal to move toward hot support. Remember that you can have consensus at either end of the spectrum.

When considering any issue look at the spectrum of possibilities rather than a binary yes/no choice. Place the high and low values from the group at different ends of the spectrum, then ask people where they fall into the range. In the above example, I would continue investigating options until there was consensus around strong support.

Example of Using Spectrums in Decision Making

Small x represents people, large X represents point of agreement. Weak agreement is when people are spread along the line, consensus is when people are grouped together.

Cost - How much should we spend? $250

<u>Medium</u>

```
_____x_____xxxx__x_____xx___x_____
$100                           $1,000
```

Frequency - How often should we do this? 2/month

<u>Weak</u>

```
___x___x_____xx_____xx__xx___x_____
monthly                      weekly
```

Feelings - How do you feel about this idea?

<u>Strong</u>

```
_____xxxxxxxxx
Lukewarm                 Enthusiastic
```

Rating Ranking, and Preference

Below, I offer a matrix intended to help compare options considering applicable criteria. The matrix allows you to use any criteria, including Virtues and Principles. Then you can weigh your available options by how they affect or are affected by each value. This offers a means of making the decision-making process more concrete and less driven by either emotional immediacy or rigid rules.

Assume you are facing a difficult situation, and you have six options available for action. You have decided on the values that apply to the situation — let's say the virtue is humility and the principles are equality, trust and the criteria of available resources.

To use the matrix in the decision-making process, consider each of your options and rate them for each value (virtue, principle or criteria) according to whether they promote (+), are neutral (0) or detract (-) from each value.

In this matrix, the hypothetical option A decreases the party's humility, promotes inequality, does not promote trust and does not use resources wisely. Option F, on the other hand, promotes all the identified values. With attributes you want to search for an option that will result in all pluses. What the options were doesn't matter at this point. The matrix is a visual example only of the types of comparisons a group find when making a decision.

Preference

Compare options using + 0 - for preferences. Everyone give each option a plus, minus or zero. Options with all pluses go forward. However a plus still doesn't tell you if you have a 51% or 99% level of support.

Options	Individual				
A	-	-	-	-	-4
B	0	-	-	0	-2
C	-	0	0	-	-2
D	+	-	0	0	0
E	+	0	+	0	2
F	+	+	+	+	4

Until you have an option that is all pluses, you may not have found the best answer. There are many different ways to use this matrix to evaluate options, including assigning numerical values to create a sliding scale or allowing each party to assign the values either in collaboration or as individuals. Just seeing the variation in how different parties in a dispute weight the values involved can be helpful to the decision-making process.

Ethics are values in action. Ethical decision making models use the values of the parties as a way to evaluate options. In the following table, each option is evaluated according to the values identified by the parties. In the A and B Options, a (-) means that the option detracts from the value, a (0) means that the option is neutral on the value and a (+) that the option promotes the value.

Until you have all pluses for any one option you may not have thought of all the options. In the C and D Options the values are ranked. In the E and F Options, each option is scored. The scoring and ranking can be used to decide where to start investigating options, with the higher scores being discussed first.

Ranking

Ranking gives a little more information than preference. Ranking can also be used to see which choice is most closely aligned with your principle.

Each person rank each option from 1 to 6. 1 = Most preferred. A is highest ranked.

Options	Individual Ranking				Total
A	1	2	1	3	7
B	5	4	3	1	13
C	2	3	2	2	9
D	3	1	4	5	13
E	6	5	6	4	21
F	4	6	5	6	21

Rating

Rating is using an objective scale to assign a numerical value to each choice. Rate each from 1 to 5. 1 = highest rated

Options	Time	Cost	Resources	People	Score
A	1	2	1	3	7
B	2	4	3	2	11
C	1	2	2	1	6
D	3	3	4	2	12
E	4	1	2	3	10
F	2	2	3	4	11

There are many other criteria that can be used to evaluate including cost, time, frequency and feeling. How often should we do this? 1=daily, 2=weekly, 3=biweekly, 4=monthly. How do you feel about this idea? 1=weak, 2=support, 3=strong

Ethics

Finally, when the principles and virtues become the criteria, the matrix becomes an ethical decision making tool.

Options	Virtues/ Principles				
	Humility	Equality	Trust	Resources	Score
A	1	2	1	3	7
B	5	4	3	1	13
C	2	3	2	2	9
D	3	1	4	5	13
E	6	5	6	4	21
F	4	6	5	6	21

Case Story — Strategic Principles out of Court, Part II

What we did was take the principles that each of the different governmental entities wanted to incorporate into the master plan and broke those down into one principle per page in a binder. We had about 120 different principles that people wanted to include when we began our discussion. There were three choices (+ - 0) for each principle:

+ Everyone agreed with the principle.

O Any one individual had a question about the principle, for example, something about its application or definition that they didn't understand.

- Any one individual had a concern about the principle, though they understood it.

We dedicated a large wall to the posting of principles and as we went through the binder, each of the principles was placed on the wall. The areas of agreement were placed high on the wall, the questions were placed in the middle and the concerns were placed low on the wall.

Consensus - agree

Questions - answer the question and move up or down

Concerns - negotiate the concerns and move up, postpone or eliminate.

On our first run through of all the principles, we ended up with full agreement on about 75% of them. Then we addressed the questions, and as each question was answered the principle either moved up or down on the wall. In other words, it either went to the consensus level or to the concerns level. Finally, we addressed all the concerns and were able to come to agree on those concerns on the spot. Using this method, we adopted 120 planning principles by consensus within an hour. This demonstrates the importance of breaking down complex issues, giving individuals choices and having constructive dialogue that addresses all the needs of the parties.

Remember!

Try to get away from yes/no votes. If you want to build consensus, offer choices and spectrums, and allow people to move along the spectrum as the idea evolves.

EXECUTE

Key	Goal	Move from	To
Execute	Action and Unity	Disparate	Unified

Taking collective action can resolve the issues, repair the relationships, promote positivity and create harmony. The group strives for consensus, however a majority vote can be taken to cause a conclusion and make the decision. Once a decision is made, it is incumbent on the entire group to act on it with unity — regardless of how many supported the idea.

Bahá'í Writings

Let deeds, not words, be your adorning. (HW)

Say: no man can attain his true station except through his justice. No power can exist except through unity. No welfare and no well-being can be attained except through consultation. (CC, vol. I, p. 93)

We love to see you at all times consorting in amity and concord within the paradise of My good-pleasure, and to inhale from your acts the fragrance of friendliness and unity, of loving-kindness and fellowship. (GL 315-316)

Make our souls dependent upon the Verses of Thy Divine Unity, our hearts cheered with the outpourings of Thy Grace, that we may unite even as the waves of one sea and become merged together as the rays of Thine effulgent Light; that our thoughts, our views, our feelings may become as one reality, manifesting the spirit of union throughout the world. (BP, p. 301)

...they may strive with all their might until universal fellowship, close and warm, and unalloyed love, and spiritual rela-

tionships, will connect all the hearts in the world....Then will conflict and dissension vanish from the face of the earth. (SWAB, 19)

If consultation among the first group of people assembled endeth in disagreement, new people should be added, after which persons to the number of the Greatest Name, or fewer or more, shall be chosen by lot. Whereupon the consultation shall be renewed, and the outcome, whatever it is, shall be obeyed. If, however, there is still disagreement, the same procedure should be repeated once more, and the decision of the majority shall prevail. He, verily, guideth whomsoever He pleaseth to the right way. (KA, p. 197)

Nothing short of the spirit of a true Bahá'í can hope to reconcile the principles of mercy and justice, of freedom and submission, of the sanctity of the right of the individual and of self-surrender, of vigilance, discretion, and prudence on the one hand, and fellowship, candor, and courage on the other. (BA, 63-64)

"....the solution, as in all such cases, is to be found through intelligent and mutual compromise...". (LOG, 638)

By this excellent method [consultation] he endeavors to arrive at unity and truth. (PUP, p. 72-73).

Indeed, it has ever been the cherished desire of our Master, Abdu'l-Bahá, that the friends in their councils, local as well as national, should by their candor, their honesty of purpose, their singleness of mind, and the thoroughness of their discussions, achieve unanimity in all things. Should this in certain cases prove impracticable the verdict of the majority should prevail, to which decision the minority must under all circumstances, gladly, spontaneously and continually, submit. (BA, 80)

___The ideal of Bahá'í consultation is to arrive at a unanimous decision (LOG, 47).

The purpose of consultation is to show that the views of several individuals are assuredly preferable to one man, even as the power of a number of men is of course greater than the power of one man. (CONS, 97)

_____*When this [unanimity] is not possible a vote must be taken...(LOG, 47)*

Every one of the friends should highly praise the other and each should regard himself as evanescent and as naught in the presence of others. All matters should be consulted upon in the meeting and whatever is the majority vote should be carried out. I swear by the one true God, it is better that all should agree on a wrong decision, than for one right vote to be singled out, inasmuch as single votes can be sources of dissension, which lead to ruin. Whereas, if in one case they take a wrong decision, in a hundred other cases they will adopt right decisions, and concord and unity are preserved. This will offset any deficiency, and will eventually lead to the righting of the wrong. (CONS 16)

It is incumbent upon every man of insight and understanding to strive to translate that which hath been written into reality and action... (Bahá'u'lláh, GL, p. 250)

Whenever it is decided to vote on a proposition all that is required is to ascertain how many of the members are in favor of it; if this is a majority of those present, the motion is carried; if it is a minority, the motion is defeated. Thus the whole question of `abstaining' does not arise in Bahá'í voting. A member who does not vote in favor of a proposition is, in effect, voting against it, even if at that moment he himself feels that he has been unable to make up his mind on the matter.(LOG, 47)

...when one is in the right in a case in dispute, and his minority prevents him from establishing this rightful matter, instead of agitating the subject , if he will humbly submit to sacrifice his position for the sake of unity and peace, God will accept that sacrifice and ere long the rightful matter will be established without any further dispute... seeking the approval of men is many times the cause of imperiling the approval of God. (SW, 45)

It is again not permitted that any one of the honored members object to or censure, whether in or out of the meeting, any decision arrived at previously, though that decision be not right, for such criticism would prevent any decision from being enforced. In short, whatsoever thing is arranged in harmony and with love and purity of motive, its result is light, and should the least trace of estrangement prevail the result shall be darkness upon darkness.... (SWAB, 88)

Bahá'ís are not required to vote on an assembly against their consciences. It is better if they submit to the majority view and make it unanimous. But they are not forced to. What they must do, however, is to abide by the majority decision, as this is what becomes effective. They must not go around undermining the assembly by saying they disagreed with the majority. In other words, they must put the Cause first and not their own opinions. He (a Spiritual Assembly member) can ask the assembly to reconsider a matter, but he has no right to force them or create in harmony because they won't change. Unanimous votes are preferable, but certainly cannot be forced upon assembly members by artificial methods such as are used by other societies. (LOG 47-48)

Each creature is the recipient of some portion of that power, and man, who contains the perfection of the mineral, the vegetable and animal, as well as his own distinctive qualities, has become the noblest of created beings. It stands written that he is made in the Image of God. Mysteries that were hidden he discovers; and secrets that were concealed he brings into the light. By Science and by Art he brings hidden powers into the region of the visible world. Man perceives the hidden law in created things and co-operates with it. (ABL, p. 23)

...the solution, as in all such cases, is to be found through intelligent and mutual compromise... ('Abdu'l-Bahá, LOG, 638)

Indeed, it has ever been the cherished desire of our Master, 'Abdu'l-Bahá, that the friends in their councils, local as well as national, should by their candor, their honesty of purpose, their singleness of mind, and the thoroughness of their discussions, achieve unanimity in all things. Should this in certain cases prove impracticable the verdict of the majority should prevail, to which decision the minority must under all circumstances, gladly, spontaneously and continually, submit. ('Abdu'l-Bahá, BA, p.80)

The friends should therefore not feel discouraged at the differences of opinion that may prevail among the members of an Assembly, for these, as experience has shown, and as the Master's words attest, fulfill a valuable function in all Assembly deliberations. But once the opinion of the majority has been ascertained, all the members should automatically and unreservedly obey it, and faithfully carry it out. Patience and restraint, however, should at all times characterize the discussions and deliberations of the elected representatives of the local community, and no fruitless and hair-splitting discussions indulged in, under any circumstances. ('Abdu'l-Bahá, CONS, pp. 104-5)

As soon as a decision is reached it becomes the decision of the whole Assembly, not merely of those members who happened to be among the majority ('Abdu'l-Bahá, LOG, p. 47).

In conclusion, the Bahá'í Writings tell us that:

- We should be known by our deeds.

- Everyone should work together to take action.

- No well-being can be attained except through consultation.

- We should become as waves of one sea.

- Connected hearts will end conflict.

- Consultation works toward unity and truth.

- The ideal is unanimity and consensus.

- A vote is only taken without consensus, only positive votes are counted.

- People can be added to the group to assist in coming to a decision.

- Everyone should unitedly support and implement the decision.

Case Story: Vocational Rehabilitation. Part I

The new director of the state agency was facing some difficult decisions. There was high employee turnover and low morale among the staff. He wanted to make some changes but was unsure of where to turn.

It is said that we only change through crisis or insight. He was wise enough to do both, to allow for the crisis to turn into an opportunity for insight. Due to the difficult situation he faced he decided to give free rein to the employees. He wanted meaningful and sustainable change.

When we met for the first time he explained the challenges he was facing. He said that he would be willing to pursue any reasonable course. I suggested a 2 day retreat for all the employees. He agreed. We set an agenda but as I always say, any agenda is only good for 5 minutes. I follow where the participants want to go; they know the way. I only help them focus their activity.

On the first day, 60 employees, without the Directors, met from across the state. We were all unsure of what to expect. I structured the program around building on what was working within the organization and then focusing on how to make those areas stronger using Appreciative Inquiry.

At the end of the first day we had distilled and prioritized a list of all the ideas for changing the organization. We had about 20 ideas with implementation plans for each of them. Everyone agreed on what needed to be done.

The Directors and Managers were joining us on the second day, what would you do?

Action and Unity

Moral excellence comes about as a result of habit. We become just by doing just acts, temperate by doing temperate acts, brave by doing brave acts. — Aristotle

No decision is complete until there has been action taken to implement it.   All decisions should have an action plan and timetable including who, what, where, when and how the decision will be carried out with a budget to meet those goals.

Action gives meaning to our words.   Without action, words would be empty promises.   With action, promises are fulfilled. With action based on spiritual values, we are bringing the attributes of God into this world.

What is effective action?

Action is the sole medium of expression for ethics. — Jane Addams

Unity is the most important aspect of action.   We must begin with unity, end with unity and use unity everywhere in between. Unity allows for higher forms of collaboration.

Unity

· is the essential truth and when so understood embraces all the virtues of the human world,

· is not merely a condition resulting from a sense of mutual goodwill and common purpose,

· is a phenomenon of creative power, whose existence becomes apparent through the effects that collective action produces,

· includes all the attributes of God,

· is built by trustworthiness, attraction (to each other and God), equality (justice) and truthfulness,

· interacts with these attributes,

· is defined as physical, emotional, intellectual and spiritual,

· is peace in action, and

· is thoughts, views and feelings (hearts) becoming one reality.

Unity allows us to take the best possible actions. Unity begins with the heart. With connected hearts we can solve any problem.

How do we take effective action?

As I noted previously, if the course of action you have selected seems to present new ethical issues, then you'll need to go back to the beginning and reevaluate each step of the process. Perhaps you have chosen the wrong option or you might have identified the problem incorrectly.

In any event, apply as criteria principles of justice, transparency and universality.

In applying the test of justice, assess your own sense of fairness by determining whether you would treat others the same in this situation or if you would wish to be treated in this way yourself.

For the test of transparency, ask yourself whether you would want your behavior reported in the press.

The test of universality asks you to assess whether you could recommend the same course of action to another in the same situation.

There are many forms of evaluation in decision-making processes. Getting to Yes (p. 4) says that any method of negotiation may be fairly judged by four criteria:

· It should produce a wise agreement.

· It should be based on objective criteria.

· It should be efficient.

· It should improve or at least not damage the relationship between the parties.

Transformative Mediation says that a resolution should result in people not just being better off, but better. In a world in which people resist change, solved problems are quickly replaced by new ones. (TM, p. 29).

It is also important that ideas be evaluated against known criteria. These criteria allow us to see the benefits of each idea. In deciding how to continue, it is important to evaluate the ideas using these questions.

· Does it allow for an improved relationship?

· Does it solve the problem completely?

· Does it solve it permanently?

· Is it possible, practical?

· Does it create another problem?

· Is it legal?

· Is it wise?

· Is it cost effective?

· How long will it take?

· How many people would be involved?

· How is this handled in your profession, organization or community?

A poor ethical decision might be...

· based on desires, theories, suppositions, unsupported conclusions, opinions, prejudices, rationalizations, and raw emotions.

· morally indefensible

· indefensible publicly

· distressing to close friends and family

· possibly illegal

· one you wish to keep secret

· one that causes you to have to rationalize to justify it

· one that makes you feel uneasy or negative about yourself or about a relationship

Key #8 - Execute

As soon as a decision is reached it becomes the decision of the whole Assembly, not merely of those members who happened to be among the majority. (LOG, 47).

Practices

Dynamic Consultation	Facilitative Mediation	World Cafe	Appreciative Inquiry	6 Hats
Execute	Agreement	Discovery	Deliver	

Facilitative Mediation - Agreement - sustainable, specific, complete and Affirmative agreements.

World Cafe - Share Collective Discoveries- Conversations held at one table reflect a pattern of wholeness that connects with the conversations at the other tables.

Appreciative Inquiry - DELIVER - People commit, offer, or request ideas to implement goals set forth in the DESIGN phase.

Rotary Four Way Test - excellent criteria

1. Is it the TRUTH?
2. Is it FAIR to all concerned?
3. Will it build GOODWILL and BETTER FRIENDSHIPS?
4. Will it be BENEFICIAL to all concerned?

Facilitation
is a constant process of
expansion and contraction.
In expansion new ideas are generated.
In contraction those ideas are explored and selected.

Skills

Always do right — this will gratify some and astonish the rest. - Mark Twain

9 Keys	9 Skills with Questions
Execute	Deeds - How can we all embrace the decision?
	Unity - How can we work as one?

Deeds

The above quotes point to the same fact: we can only show ethics through action. Ethical action is the result of value-based decision-making. Taking the appropriate action in an ethical dilemma is often difficult. The final step involves strengthening your ego to allow you to carry out your plan.

After implementing your course of action, it is good practice to follow up on the situation to assess whether your actions had the anticipated effect and to judge the consequences. This step often requires the supporting character traits of courage or self-control.

Unity

It is important to realize that different professionals may implement different courses of action in the same situation. There is rarely one right answer to a complex ethical dilemma. However, if you follow a systematic model, you can be assured that you will be able to give an ethical explanation for the course of action you have taken and know that you have done everything possible to do the right thing. Following this model will help to ensure that all ethical conditions have been met.

If you have strong consensus around a well devised plan, you will succeed. All we need to do is to shift that spiritual image into the material world.

Case Story: Vocational Rehabilitation, Part II

What happened when the bosses joined the group?

The following morning the directors joined the group. The employees presented their ideas and the directors asked questions for clarification. To everyone's surprise, the director's accepted all of the employees' ideas. The employees formed task forces around each idea and began to work on implementing them.

One idea stood out from all the rest. I always tell organizations that you have to work within the box of the organization; you can't decide to do something that is not part of your goals and objectives, and something that is outside of your span of control. Apparently I forgot to tell them, because one of their ideas was to change state law. The state law had specified a number of practices and descriptions that no longer applied to their agency. However no one dared to change it because of the politics and bureaucracy involved.

Well, the group rewrote the law and submitted it to the legislature. The legislature passed the law.

I spoke to a conference of the same group three years later and most of the task forces formed as part of this meeting were continuing to function. This was because people were given the support and encouragement to bring about meaningful change.

Remember

Unity in the decision leads to action, however action doesn't always lead to unity.

Only take action when there is strong consensus.

EXAMINE

Key	Goal	Move from	To
Examine	Reflection and Growth	Criticism	Appreciation

Reflect on your decisions and actions to improve them in the future. Consider the effects of your consultation in relation to the implementation of the decision. Look for ways to improve upon your action in the future.

Bahá'í Writings

Baha'u'llah says there is a sign (from God) in every phenomenon: the sign of the intellect is contemplation and the sign of contemplation is silence, because it is impossible for a man to do two things at one time he cannot both speak and meditate.

It is an axiomatic fact that while you meditate you are speaking with your own spirit. In that state of mind you put certain questions to your spirit and the spirit answers: the light breaks forth and the reality is revealed.

Through the faculty of meditation man attains to eternal life; through it he receives the breath of the Holy Spirit the bestowal of the Spirit is given in reflection and meditation.

The spirit of man is itself informed and strengthened during meditation; through it affairs of which man knew nothing are unfolded before his view. Through it he receives Divine inspiration, through it he receives heavenly food.

Meditation is the key for opening the doors of mysteries. In that state man abstracts himself: in that state man withdraws himself from all outside objects; in that subjective mood he is immersed in the ocean of spiritual life and can unfold the secrets of things in themselves. To illustrate this, think of man as endowed with two kinds of sight; when the power of insight is being used the outward power of vision does not see.

This faculty of meditation frees man from the animal nature, discerns the reality of things, puts man in touch with God.

This faculty brings forth from the invisible plane the sciences and arts. Through the meditative faculty inventions are made possible, colossal undertakings are carried out; through it governments can run smoothly. Through this faculty man enters into the very Kingdom of God.

Nevertheless some thoughts are useless to man; they are like waves moving in the sea without result. But if the faculty of meditation is bathed in the inner light and characterized with divine attributes, the results will be confirmed. (PT, p. 79)

Therefore I say that man must travel in the way of God. Day by day he must endeavor to become better, his belief must increase and become firmer, his good qualities and his turning to God must be greater, the fire of his love must flame more brightly; then day by day he will make progress, for to stop advancing is the means of going back. The bird when he flies soars ever higher and higher, for as soon as he stops flying he will come down. Every day, in the morning when arising you should compare today with yesterday and see in what condition you are. If you see your belief is stronger and your heart more occupied with God and your love increased and your freedom from the world greater (detachment) then thank God and ask for the increase of these qualities. You must begin to pray and repent for all that you have done that is wrong and you must implore and ask for help and assistance that you may become better than yesterday so that you may continue to make progress. 'Abdu'l-Bahá, in Star of the West 8, no. 6 (24 June 1917), p. 68.

The friends have begun to appreciate that not all answers can be tied down in advance but are garnered through experience. Meetings of consultation held at the cluster level serve to raise awareness of possibilities and generate enthusiasm. Here, free from the demands of formal decision-making, participants reflect on experience gained, share insights, explore approaches and acquire a better understanding of how each can contribute to achieving the aim of the Plan. In many cases, such interaction leads to consensus on a set of short-term goals, both individual and collective. Learning in action is becoming the outstanding feature of the emerging mode of operation. (ITC, Building Momentum - ITC 2003-04-23, p. 17)

True education releases capacities, develops analytical abilities, confidence, will, and goal-setting competencies, and instills the vision that will enable them to become self-motivating change agents, serving the best interests of the community. Individuals should be skilled in the art of consultative decision-making and empowered with a sense of their own dignity and worth. They should understand their positions as members of both a local community and the world community, and they must believe their lives can make a difference.   (Bahá'í International Community, 1990 Mar 08)

In conclusion, the Bahá'í Writings tell us that:

One hour's reflection is preferable to seventy years of pious worship. (KI, p. 237)

- Reflection needs silence

- Reflect on your actions to become better

- Reflection is conversation with our spirit

- Reflection is a building block of consensus

- Reflection and action are partners in learning.

Case Story — Two Couples and a Dog, Part I

There are several notable times when I've used the reflection process. One occasion was with spouses who had lived next door to each other for a number of years. They were having problems with a barking dog and I think we all understand that there won't be peace in the world until we teach dogs to only bark at appropriate times.

These neighbors were literally yelling at one another in mediation, which is fairly unusual. In most Dynamic Consultations, I'm used to the parties being fairly well-behaved once they agree to sit down in the Dynamic Consultation room. If anything, they start out being a little too reserved and quiet. Not so with these folks. They came in assaulting one another verbally and I had put an end to it.

I asked each couple to go to a separate room and to sit down and reflect on what they would like to get out of the consultation. I asked them what they were willing to do to help resolve it and what they would like to ask their neighbors to consider doing. After fifteen minutes, I invited them back into the Dynamic Consultation room.

What would they do during their time apart?

Reflection and Growth

Our purpose in reflecting is to grow spiritually. This is our formula for reflection and this is why we should bring ourselves to account each day. When we arise each morning, we should take account of our lives and each day should be better than the last.

Mature ethical reasoning is generally defined as that which recognizes the concerns of others, as opposed to less mature thinking, which focuses solely on the selfish aims of the individual or group. Practicing ethical reflection is a necessary requirement to promote maturity in ethical thinking. The application of a practical ethical decision-making framework assists in the reflection process. The framework includes virtues, principles and reciprocal ethics as behavior goals.

Process reflection is one of the least used and most potent tools of consultation. Below are examples of questions that might be asked at the end of a meeting. The answers should be recorded and the next meeting should open with the responses from the prior meeting. Steps should then be taken to improve the consultative process at the current meeting based on the responses.

Participatory Decision Making says that groups need to understand and recognize how they work together. Each consultation should end with a discussion of what part of the process worked and what needs to be changed. The next session should always begin with this critique as a reminder to the group. The group can then truly evolve and improve its consultative process.

Practicing ethical reflection is a necessary process for promoting maturity in ethical thinking. Reflection allows us to consider questions in a deeper and more personal way. It allows us to step back from a situation, an experience or even a possibility, and consider our role in it.

Philosopher Michael Boylan has brought up the importance of Personal Worldview Imperative which states that, "All people must develop a single, comprehensive and internally coherent worldview that is good and that we strive to act out in our daily lives." Boylan posits that we must reflect on whether our lives would be recognized as good by any rational person. He believes that this personal self-reflection will lead to positive, ethical behavior.

In reflecting on your actions, there are several questions that are important to ask. First, what were you hoping to accomplish? What were your material and spiritual goals?

Just as prayer and action go together, so do material and spiritual goals. Consider your accomplishments and consider what you would do the same and what you would do differently. Reflect on past decisions and compare outcomes with the consequences that were anticipated at the time of the choice. This step can help reinforce the value of practicing value-based decision-making.

Next, what spiritual qualities, values and indicators were demonstrated? Look for increased levels of trustworthiness, unity and equality.

Key # 9 - Examine

One hour's reflection is preferable to seventy years of pious worship. (KI, p. 237)

Practices

Dynamic Consultation	Facilitative Mediation	World Cafe	Appreciative Inquiry	6 Hats
Examine				

While reflection is certainly supported by the group processes we have presented, Dynamic Consultation is the only practice that presents it as part of the process.

Skills

Never doubt that a small group of thoughtful, committed citizens can change the world. Indeed, it is the only thing that ever has. --Margaret Mead

9 Keys	9 Skills with Questions
Examine	Reflection - What worked? Enhance - How can we improve next time?

Reflection

In considering our conflict resolution process we should ask ourselves:

1.   What worked (pluses +)?

2.   What could be changed (deltas)?

3.   How do we feel about our conflict resolution?

4.   What did we learn from this?

5.   What do we want to do next time?

Practicing ethical reflection is a necessary process for promoting maturity in ethical thinking. Reflection allows us to consider questions in a deeper and more personal way. It allows us to step back from a situation, an experience or even a possibility, and consider our role in it.

Business consultant Stephen Covey says that between any stimulus and response is a choice. Reflection is the bridge between stimulus and response that leads to a better, deeper, different life. During reflection we listen for the response to these questions and take time to ponder and meditate. We detach ourselves from the situation, quiet our minds, consider multiple perspectives and think about who we want to be.

Philosopher Michael Boylan has brought up the importance of Personal Worldview Imperative which states that, "All people must develop a single, comprehensive and internally coherent worldview that is good and that we strive to act out in our daily lives." Boylan posits that we must reflect on whether our lives would be recognized as good by any rational person. He believes that this personal self-reflection will lead to Affirmative, ethical behavior.

Enhance

In reflecting on your actions, there are several questions that are important to ask. First, what were you hoping to accomplish? What were your material and ethical goals?

Just as reflection and action go together, so do material and ethical goals. Consider your accomplishments and consider what you would do the same and what you would do differently. Reflect on past decisions and compare outcomes with the consequences that were anticipated at the time of the choice. This step can help reinforce the value of practicing value-based decision-making.

Next, what ethical qualities, values and indicators were demonstrated? Look for increased levels of trustworthiness, unity and equality.

Finally, reflect on your life in relation to your goals and actions. What are you planning to do? What have you accomplished? Have you grown ethically?

Group Reflection

Group reflection is one of the least used and most potent tools of conflict resolution.   Below are examples of questions that might be asked at the end of a meeting.   The answers should be recorded and the next meeting should open with the responses from the prior meeting.   Steps should then be taken to improve the conflict resolution process at the current meeting based on the responses.

Failure

Give me a fruitful error any time, full of seeds, bursting with its own corrections.   You can keep your sterile truth for yourself.   ~Vilfredo Pareto

You have to be honest in your reflection and recognize when something needs to be improved. If everything is fine, then nothing will ever change. You learn and grow much more through failure than through success. Charlie Brown must be the wisest man in the world.

I have always found that I learned much more when I wasn't able to help parties reach an agreement, because I tried everything I could. Reciprocal Negotiation in the chapter on Expand was a clear example of having to devise a new course when nothing was working.

Case Story — Two Couples and a Dog, Part II

During the time apart they'd had meaningful conversations as couples, and were much more prepared to proceed. The first thing one neighbor was willing to do was to apologize. He said he would like to do so now. Obviously, that changed the entire tone of the discussion, but more than that, it gave all parties the ability to take responsibility for their own actions. They proceeded to apologize for all of their actions and to sincerely say they wanted to work together to improve the situation.

At that point, I'm sure both couples took a closer look at the list they had generated and very selectively went through and brought up the remaining issues. They had established a human bond and now they could work through any difficulty.

In considering the central question of virtue ethics (Who shall I be?), one must first begin with the question, "Who do I want to be?" Ultimately this internal decision will lead you on a path to develop the character traits that you feel are important. This is commonly practiced through reflection, and such methods as meditating and journal writing. One of the greatest goals we can assume in life is the formation of our character, and ultimately the one way we can develop an answer to "The Big Question" is through the art of reflection.

Remember

Take time to reflect on your decisions.

Ask what worked and what do we want to change.

Look to improve each day.

Learn from your failures.

SUMMARY AND CONCLUSION

Bahá'í consultation is at the very foundation of modern group process. It contains the values and attributes necessary for optimal group performance. This workbook has hopefully demonstrated how skills and techniques from compatible group processes can be used in a Bahá'í consultative environment to enhance group performance, and to show how Bahá'í consultative principles can be used in secular settings.

Dynamic Consultation helps you look at your life through an ethical lens. Ethics, like faith, works to approach perfection, but is always open to improvement. The following steps summarize the Dynamic Consultation model. While they are presented as a process, any step can be used independently at any time.

- Create guidelines that are rational and loving.

- Understand your feelings and those of others. Feelings tell us why something is important.

- Look at the situation from your perspective and gather information first hand rather than through the knowledge of others. Then, listen to others and understand their perspectives.

- Frame the issue in a way that is positive, neutral, future focused, looks at the big picture and allows for the possibility of a solution.

- Consider the virtues you want to develop.

- Select the appropriate principles for the situation.

- Look at the reciprocal obligations of the choices. Are you giving an equal or greater share?

- Generate a wide range of positive, productive choices.

- Evaluate the choices based on wise criteria

- Take unified action.

- Reflect on your ethical choices and look to grow and improve each day.

Dynamic Consultation is about connecting being with doing. It is where our thoughts, words and deeds are harmonized. The appearance of virtue and the adherence to principles are not unintended consequences, but intentional will and action put at the forefront of our decision-making process. Ethical actions are the outcome of value-based decisions.

Truly, Dynamic Consultations are divinely inspired. They are based on the noblest qualities of humanity. They allow us to use our free will to manifest our highest qualities. While Dynamic Consultations are based on truthfulness and trustworthiness — two of the foundational virtues — the Dynamic Consultation Model includes spiritual and practical attributes, and allows for a wide range of action.

Our action is manifested through the things we do for others in this world. The only things that we take with us from this life are the spiritual "treasures" we accrue here — our relationship with God, with ourselves, with other souls, the positive attributes we have developed and the good we have done. Good deeds done with an intentional mindset will allow us to more fully explore and more thoroughly develop our spiritual selves.

Dynamic Consultation is beliefs, virtues, thoughts, principles and words in action. The combination results in personal transformation and relational growth because it provides the opportunity to develop divine attributes.

Dynamic Consultation connects the spiritual and material through prayer and action. If we only reflect upon the spiritual world and do not act on it, we have not fulfilled our destiny.

Dynamic Consultation is consistent in that it leads to actions that support our deepest beliefs and are sustainable because they provide long-term solutions.

The Dynamic Consultation process gets more robust with every use and becomes easier with each application. It provides clear guidelines and helps you toward a decision-making process that can serve as an example to others. It allows once-dissenting individuals to speak with one voice, enables decision-making bodies to present unified and consistent responses to all supplicants and helps each of us leave the ethical woodpile higher than we found it. It encourages you to take the road less traveled by.

I hope this book has inspired you to reflect on and take action toward using a values-driven approach for making better choices.

Bibliography

Bahá'í Writings

HW: Bahá'u'lláh. The Hidden Words of Bahá'u'lláh. Wilmette, Ill.: Bahá'í Publishing Trust, Wilmette, 1963.

KA: _____ . Kitab-i-Aqdás. Wilmette, Ill.: Bahá'í Publishing Trust, 1993.

GL: _____ . Gleanings from the Writings of Bahá'u'lláh. Wilmette, Ill.:Bahá'í Publishing Trust, 1976.

KI: _____. Kitab-i-Iqán, Wilmette, Ill.:Bahá'í Publishing Trust, 1976.

TAB: _____. Tablets of Bahá'u'lláh, Wilmette, Ill.:Bahá'í Publishing Trust, 1976.

ABL: 'Abdu'l-Bahá . 'Abdu'l-Bahá in London,

CC: _____. The Compilation of Compilations.

CONS: _____. CONSULTATION: A COMPILATION, Compiled by the Research Department of the Universal House of Justice

ED: _____. Education, From a Tablet - translated from the Persian.

FWU: _____. Foundations of World Unity, National Spiritual Assembly of the United States. Consultation: A Compilation. Wilmette, Ill.: Bahá'í Publishing Trust, .

HQ: _____. Huqúqu'lláh

LOG: _____ . In Lights of Guidance. Ed. Helen Hornby Bassett. New Delhi: Bahá'í Publishing Trust, 1994.

PT: _____. Paris Talks,

SAQ: _____. Some Answered Questions, Wilmette, Ill.: Bahá'í Publishing Trust, 1982

SW: _____. Star of the West

SWAB: _____. Selections from the Writings of 'Abdu'l-Bahá. Haifa, Israel: Bahá'í World Center, 1978.

PUP: _____. The Promulgation of Universal Peace. Wilmette, Ill.: Bahá'í Publishing Trust, 1982.

WT: _____. Will and Testament. Wilmette, Ill.: Bahá'í Publishing Trust, 1982

ADJ: Shoghi Effendi. The Advent of Divine Justice.

BA: _____. Bahá'í Administration

BP: Baha'i Prayers. A Selection of prayers revealed by Baha'u'llah, the Bab, and Abdu'l-Baha 2002, National Spiritual Assembly of the Baha'is of the United States

IRF: Individual Rights and Freedoms, Universal House of Justice, 1985.

OCF: _____. One Common Faith, commissioned by the Universal House of Justice.

PWP: _____. The Promise of World Peace, The Universal House of Justice, 1985

BM: Bahá'í International Teaching Centre . Building Momentum ITC 2003-04-23

VSD: Valuing Spirituality in Development. Baha'i International Community, Feb 18 , 1998.

BNE: Baha'u'llah and the New Era. Esslemont, J.E. National Spiritual Assembly of the Baha'is of the United States, 1980.

UHJ: Universal House of Justice, 1990 Ridvan letter

GLSA: Guidelines for Local Spiritual Assemblies. National Spiritual Assembly of the Baha'is of the United States

Positive Psychology

Bower, B. Sleeper Effects: Slumber may fortify memory, stir insights. Sciencenews.org

Frankl, Viktor. Man's Search for Meaning,. Beacon Press, 2006

Fredrickson, B. L., & Losada, M. F. (2005). Positive Affect and the Complex Dynamics of Human Flourishing. American Psychologist, 60(7), 678-686.

Keyes CLM and Haidt J, eds. Flourishing: Positive Psychology and the Life Well Lived (American Psychological Association, 2002).

Kitchener, K. S., (1984). Intuition, critical evaluation, and ethical principles: The foundation for ethical decisions in counseling psychology. *Counseling Psychologist, 12*, 43-55.

Krentzman, A. R. (2012, September 17). Review of the Application of Positive Psychology to Substance Use, Addiction, and Recovery Research. Psychology of Addictive Behaviors. Advance online publication

Mednick, S.C., et.al. The restorative effect of naps on perceptual deterioration, Nature Neuroscience 5, 677–681 (July 2002)

Peterson, Christopher (2006). A Primer in Positive Psychology. Oxford University Press.

Schneider, K. (2011). Toward a Humanistic Positive Psychology. Existential Analysis: Journal Of The Society For Existential Analysis, 22(1), 32-38.

Seligman, Martin E.P.; Csikszentmihalyi, Mihaly (2000). "Positive Psychology: An Introduction". American Psychologist 55 (1): 5–14.

Siang-Yang, T. (2006). Applied Positive Psychology: Putting Positive Psychology into Practice. Journal Of Psychology & Christianity, 25(1), 68-73.

Processes

Bush, R.A.B., & Folger, J.P. (1994) The promise of mediation: Responding to conflict through empowerment and recognition. San Francisco, CA: Jossey Bass.

Cochran, Alice C. (2004) Roberta's Rules of Order. Jossey-Bass

De Bono, Edward (1996) Six Thinking Hats. Boston: Little, Brown and Company.

Fisher, Roger & Ury, William (1991) Getting to Yes. New York: Penguin Books

Gray, John (2008) Why Mars and Venus Collide: Improving Relationships by Understanding How Men and Women Cope Differently with Stress. Harper Perennial

Goleman, Daniel (1995) Emotional Intelligence, New York: Bantam Publishing Company.

Harrison, O. Open Space,

Kaner, Sam (1996). Facilitator's Guide to Participatory Decision-Making. Gabriola Island, BC: New Society.

Lehrer, Jason. (2011) Imagine: How Creativity Works.

Martinetz, C. Appreciative Inquiry as an Organizational Development Tool, (2002).

McCarthy, Bernice (1987). The 4Mat System: Teaching to Learning Styles with Right/Left Mode Techniques. Barrington, IL: Excel.

Mennonite Conciliation Service, Guide to Mediation and Facilitation, www.mcc.org/mcs.html

Schwarz, Roger M. (1994) The Skilled Facilitator. San Francisco: Jossey Bass.

Sibbet, David (2002) Best Practices for Facilitation, San Francisco: Grove Consultants   International. 800-494-7683, www.grove.-com

Surowiecki, James. (2005). The Wisdom of Crowds: Why the Many Are Smarter Than the Few and How Collective Wisdom Shapes Business, Economies, Societies and Nations. Doubleday.

Weisbord, Marvin R. & Janoff, Sandra, Future search (1995), San Francisco: Berrett-Koehler.

World Cafe, www.worldcafe.org

A Comparison of Mediation Processes

Process	Dynamic Consultation	Facilitative Mediation	Transformative Mediation
Source	Baha'i	Getting to Yes	Promise of Mediation
Perspective	Oneness of Mankind	Get what you want	Relational Vision
Principles	Truth, Love	Separate the people from the Problem	Moral Growth
Process	Spiritual Conference	Problem Solving	Recognition Empowerment
Behaviors	Love, Patience Understanding	Explicit	Strong and Caring
Outcomes	Unity through God's Spirit	Objective / Efficient	Transformation

A Comparison of Faith Based Approaches

Process	Dynamic Consultation	Meeting	8 Fold Path
Source	Baha'i	Quaker	Buddhism
Perspective	Oneness of Mankind	Seek Divine Will	Right Mind
Principles	Truth, Love	Awareness, Unity	Right Understanding
Process	Spiritual Conference	No set point of view	Right Effort
Behaviors	Love, Patience Understanding	Meekness	Right Attitude, Speech
Outcomes	Unity through God's Spirit	Sense of Meeting	Right Action

BIOGRAPHY

TRIP BARTHEL, M.A.C.R. (Antioch Univ.), has been teaching and practicing mediation and facilitation around the world since 1997. He has taught at the National Judicial College, University of Nevada (Reno), JiaoTong University (Shanghai), Shanghai University of Political Science and Law, and Shivaji University in Pune, India. He has given training programs in Hong Kong, Philippines, Thailand, Malaysia, India, Russia, Czech Republic and England. He was the Founder and past Executive Director (1999-2009), Neighborhood Mediation Center, Reno, Nevada. Trip has conducted over 400 mediations, 50 arbitrations and trained over 3,000 people in courses ranging from 2-40 hours. Trip is past President of the Nevada Dispute Resolution Coalition and a member of Association for Conflict Resolution. Trip serves on the Advisory Board for Mediators Beyond Borders and the Asia Pacific Mediation Forum.

In this book, as well as in all his professional work, Trip is inspired by the practices of the Bahá'í Faith, whose values are at the core of his beliefs. The Bahá'í Faith offers clear guidelines for how people can talk and work together. Bahá'ís are asked to continually strive to do "that which is praiseworthy" as we raise our families, participate in our communities, educate ourselves, and serve humanity.

Trip enjoys conducting imaginative and interactive teaching and training experiences at conferences, schools and around the world. You can contact him at trip1844@gmail.com or at www.5kth.com/5k. The picture on the back cover was taken at the United Nations NGO Conference in September, 2006.

Zena Zumeta

Paul Lample on framing

Jonah ~~Leir~~ Lehrer
(brainstorming ~~doesn't~~ work)